Lesson Plans

McDougal Littell

THE LANGUAGE OF
LITERATURE

AMERICAN LITERATURE

D1303578

CURRICULUM

Weeks-Townsend Memorial Library
Union College
Barbourville, KY 40906

McDougal Littell
A HOUGHTON MIFFLIN COMPANY
Evanston, Illinois • Boston • Dallas

CUR
62
ML
11
2006
LP

Permission is hereby granted to teachers to reprint or photocopy in classroom quantities
the pages or sheets in this work that carry a McDougal Littell copyright notice. These
pages are designed to be reproduced by teachers for use in their classes with accompanying
McDougal Littell material, provided each copy made shows the copyright notice. Such
copies may not be sold, and further distribution is expressly prohibited. Except as
authorized above, prior written permission must be obtained from McDougal Littell
Inc. to reproduce or transmit this work or portions thereof in any other form or by any
other electronic or mechanical means, including any information storage or retrieval
system, unless expressly permitted by federal copyright law. Address inquiries to Manager,
Rights and Permissions, McDougal Littell Inc., P. O. Box 1667, Evanston, Illinois 60204.

ISBN 0-618-06018-9

Copyright © 2001 by McDougal Littell Inc.
Box 1667, Evanston, Illinois 60204
All rights reserved. Printed in the United States of America.

5 6 7 8 9 10 - MDO - 10 09 08 07 06 05

Contents

The World on the Turtle's Back

Core Objectives
- Understand and appreciate a creation myth
- Identify causes and effects

Integrating Skills

Grammar
- Diagnostic:
  Parts of Speech
- Parts of Speech

Vocabulary
- Context Clues

Preparing to Read
____ Connect to Your Life
____ Build Background
____ Vocabulary Preview: Context Clues   ❑ Unit One Resource Book: Words to Know SkillBuilder, p. 11
____ Focus Your Reading
____ Literary Analysis: Creation Myths   ❑ Unit One Resource Book: Literary Analysis SkillBuilder, p. 10
____ Active Reading: Causes and Effects   ❑ Unit One Resource Book: Active Reading SkillBuilder, p. 9

Teaching the Literature
❑ PE pp. 24–32
____ Reading the Selection   ❑ Unit One Resource Book: Summary, p. 8

Thinking Through the Literature
____ Connect to the Literature
____ Think Critically   ❑ Reading and Critical Thinking Transparencies, T1, T49, T51
____ Extend Interpretations
____ Literary Analysis: Creation Myths   ❑ Literary Analysis Transparencies, T24

Choices and Challenges

Writing Options
____ Essay on Harmony
____ Opinion Essay
____ Alternate Ending

Activities and Explorations
____ Oral Storytelling
____ Narrative Pictographs
____ Food Chain Diagram

Inquiry and Research
____ Creation Stories Compared

Vocabulary in Action
____ Assessment Practice

Art Connection
____ Every Picture Tells a Story

Copyright © McDougal Littell Inc.

The World on the Turtle's Back

Teaching Options (from Teacher's Edition)

Mini Lessons

Preteaching Vocabulary
____ Context Clues

Grammar
____ Diagnostic: Parts of Speech   ❑ Grammar Transparencies and Copymasters, C61
____ Parts of Speech

Viewing and Representing
Art Appreciation
____ *Creation Legend* by Tom Two-Arrows

Assessment

____ Selection Quiz   ❑ Unit One Resource Book: Selection Quiz, p. 12
____ Selection Test   ❑ Formal Assessment: Selection Test, pp. 7–8
____ Test Generator

Homework Assignments	Other Teaching Materials

Copyright © McDougal Littell Inc.

Song of the Sky Loom / Hunting Song

Core Objectives
- Understand and appreciate sacred songs
- Appreciate author's use of repetition
- Apply strategies for reading Native American songs

Integrating Skills

Grammar
- Plurals from Possessives

Vocabulary
- Using Context Clues

Preparing to Read
____ Connect to Your Life
____ Build Background
____ Focus Your Reading
    Literary Analysis: Repetition   ❑ Unit One Resource Book: Literary Analysis SkillBuilder, p. 14
    Active Reading: Strategies for Reading Native   ❑ Unit One Resource Book: Active Reading SkillBuilder, p. 13
      American Songs

Teaching the Literature
____ Reading the Selection   ❑ PE pp. 33–38

Thinking Through the Literature
____ Connect to the Literature
____ Think Critically   ❑ Reading and Critical Thinking Transparencies, T15, T32
____ Extend Interpretations
____ Literary Analysis: Repetition   ❑ Literary Analysis Transparencies, T24

Choices and Challenges

Writing Options
____ Definition Essay
____ Siren Song
____ Reflective Essay

Activities and Explorations
____ Oral Reading
____ Visual Storytelling

Inquiry and Research
____ Mapping the Music
____ Thrill of the Hunt
____ Hear My Song

Copyright © McDougal Littell Inc.

Song of the Sky Loom / Hunting Song

Teaching Options (from Teacher's Edition)

Mini Lessons

Vocabulary Strategy
___ Using Context Clues

❑ Vocabulary Transparencies and Copymasters, C18

Grammar
___ Forming and Distinguishing Plurals from Possessives

❑ Grammar Transparencies and Copymasters, C64

Viewing and Representing
Art Appreciation
___ *Born Free* by Edwin Salomon

Assessment

___ Selection Test
___ Test Generator

❑ Formal Assessment: Selection Test, p. 9

Homework Assignments

_____

_____

_____

_____

_____

Other Teaching Materials

_____

_____

_____

_____

Copyright © McDougal Littell Inc.

Coyote Stories

Core Objectives
- Understand and appreciate trickster tales
- Use strategies for reading trickster tales

Integrating Skills

Grammar
- Capitalization
- Different Types of Sentences

Vocabulary
- Context Clues
- Expanding Vocabulary Through Wide Reading

Preparing to Read
____ Connect to Your Life
____ Build Background
____ Focus Your Reading
    Literary Analysis: Trickster Tales
    Active Reading: Strategies for Reading
      Trickster Tales

❏ Unit One Resource Book: Literary Analysis SkillBuilder, p. 18
❏ Unit One Resource Book: Active Reading SkillBuilder, p. 17

Teaching the Literature
____ Reading the Selection

❏ PE pp. 39–47
❏ Unit One Resource Book: Summary, pp. 15–16

Thinking Through the Literature
____ Connect to the Literature
____ Think Critically
____ Extend Interpretations
____ Literary Analysis: Trickster Tales

❏ Reading and Critical Thinking Transparencies, T15, T48

❏ Literary Analysis Transparencies, T24

Choices and Challenges
Writing Options
____ Magazine Article
____ Updated Trickster Tale

Activities and Explorations
____ Creating Pantomime
____ Coyote on Video

Copyright © McDougal Littell Inc.

Teaching Options (from Teacher's Edition)

Mini Lessons

Vocabulary Strategy
____ Using Context Clues and Footnotes
____ Expanding Vocabulary Through Wide
Reading
    ❑ Vocabulary Transparencies and Copymasters, C19

Grammar
____ Capitalization of Proper Nouns and
Adjectives
    ❑ Grammar Transparencies and Copymasters, C142

____ Identifying Different Types of Sentences
    ❑ Grammar Transparencies and Copymasters, C74

Viewing and Representing
Art Appreciation
____ *Nootka Wood Whale Effigy Rattle*
by anonymous
____ *Mask for a Coyote Dance* by anonymous

Informal Assessment
____ Arrange Events in Sequential Order

Assessment
____ Selection Quiz
    ❑ Unit One Resource Book: Selection Quiz, p. 19
____ Selection Test
    ❑ Formal Assessment: Selection Test, pp. 11–12
____ Test Generator

Homework Assignments

_____

_____

_____

_____

Other Teaching Materials

_____

_____

_____

Copyright © McDougal Littell Inc.

The Man to Send Rain Clouds

Core Objectives
- Understand and appreciate a short story
- Recognize author's use of conflict
- Make inferences based on information presented in a story

Integrating Skills

Grammar
- Capitalizing First Word of a Sentence

Vocabulary
- Context Clues

Preparing to Read
____ Comparing Literature
____ Build Background
____ Vocabulary Preview: Context Clues   ❑ Unit One Resource Book: Words to Know SkillBuilder, p. 23
____ Focus Your Reading
     Literary Analysis: Conflict   ❑ Unit One Resource Book: Literary Analysis SkillBuilder, p. 22
     Active Reading: Making Inferences   ❑ Unit One Resource Book: Active Reading SkillBuilder, p. 21

Teaching the Literature
____ Reading the Selection   ❑ PE pp. 48–54
                     ❑ Unit One Resource Book: Summary, p. 20

Thinking Through the Literature
____ Connect to the Literature
____ Think Critically   ❑ Reading and Critical Thinking Transparencies, T7
____ Extend Interpretations
____ Literary Analysis: Conflict   ❑ Literary Analysis Transparencies, T14

Choices and Challenges

Writing Options
____ Performance Review
____ Descriptions of Rites

Activities and Explorations
____ Illustrative Scene
____ Points of Comparison

Vocabulary in Action
____ Related Words

Author Activity
____ Silko the Storyteller

Copyright © McDougal Littell Inc.

The Man to Send Rain Clouds

Teaching Options (from Teacher's Edition)

Mini Lessons

Preteaching Vocabulary

____ Context Clues

Grammar

____ Capitalizing First Word of Sentence   ❑ Grammar Transparencies and Copymasters, C146

Viewing and Representing

Art Appreciation

____ *Between Heaven and Earth; Earth and Sky*
by Frank LaPena

Cross Curricular Link

History

____ Laguna Pueblo

Informal Assessment

____ Identifying Implied Main Idea

Assessment

____ Selection Quiz   ❑ Unit One Resource Book: Selection Quiz, p. 24

____ Selection Test   ❑ Formal Assessment: Selection Test, pp. 13–14

____ Test Generator

Homework Assignments

_____

_____

_____

_____

_____

Other Teaching Materials

_____

_____

_____

_____

Copyright © McDougal Littell Inc.

The Way to Rainy Mountain

Core Objectives
- Understand and appreciate a personal narrative
- Appreciate author's use of setting
- Understand the structure of a personal narrative

Integrating Skills

Grammar
- Pronouns
- Predicates

Vocabulary
- Using Reference Materials
- Connotations

Preparing to Read
___ Comparing Literature
___ Build Background
___ Vocabulary Preview: Using Reference
　　　Materials
___ Focus Your Reading
　　　Literary Analysis: Setting
　　　Active Reading: Understanding Structure

❑ Unit One Resource Book: Words to Know SkillBuilder, p. 28

❑ Unit One Resource Book: Literary Analysis SkillBuilder, p. 27
❑ Unit One Resource Book: Active Reading SkillBuilder, p. 26

Teaching the Literature
___ Reading the Selection

❑ PE pp. 55–63
❑ Unit One Resource Book: Summary, p. 25

Thinking Through the Literature
___ Connect to the Literature
___ Think Critically
___ Extend Interpretations
___ Literary Analysis: Setting

❑ Reading and Critical Thinking Transparencies, T6, T17

❑ Literary Analysis Transparencies, T13

Choices and Challenges

Writing Options
___ A Fitting Eulogy
___ Points of Comparison

Activities and Explorations
___ Points of Comparison

Vocabulary in Action
___ Assessment Practice

Copyright © McDougal Littell Inc.

The Way to Rainy Mountain

Teaching Options (from Teacher's Edition)

Mini Lessons

Preteaching Vocabulary
____ Using Reference Materials

Vocabulary Strategy
____ Interpreting Connotations   ❑ Vocabulary Transparencies and Copymasters, C26

Grammar
____ Pronouns   ❑ Grammar Transparencies and Copymasters, C65
____ Compound and Simple Predicates   ❑ Grammar Transparencies and Copymasters, C77

Speaking and Listening
____ Presenting Interpretations

Cross Curricular Link

Science
____ The Roots of the Plains

Informal Assessment
____ Arranging Events in Sequential Order

Assessment
____ Selection Quiz   ❑ Unit One Resource Book: Selection Quiz, p. 29
____ Selection Test   ❑ Formal Assessment: Selection Test, pp. 15–16
____ Part Test   ❑ Formal Assessment: Unit One, Part 1 Test, pp. 17–18
____ Test Generator

Homework Assignments

_____
_____
_____
_____
_____

Other Teaching Materials

_____
_____
_____
_____
_____

Copyright © McDougal Littell Inc.

from La Relación

Core Objectives
■ Read a nonfiction report
■ Examine how audience influences the author
■ Use text organizers

Integrating Skills

Grammar
■ Simple Sentences
■ Review Parts of Speech

Vocabulary
■ Using Context Clues
■ Applying Prefix and Root Word Meanings

Preparing to Read
____ Connect to Your Life
____ Build Background
____ Vocabulary Preview: Using Context Clues ❑ Unit One Resource Book: Words to Know SkillBuilder, p. 34
____ Focus Your Reading
　　　 Literary Analysis: Audience ❑ Unit One Resource Book: Literary Analysis SkillBuilder, p. 33
　　　 Active Reading: Using Text Organizers ❑ Unit One Resource Book: Active Reading SkillBuilder, p. 32

Teaching the Literature
____ Reading the Selection
❑ PE pp. 72–80
❑ Unit One Resource Book: Summary, p. 31

Thinking Through the Literature
____ Connect to the Literature
____ Think Critically ❑ Reading and Critical Thinking Transparencies, T16, T37
____ Extend Interpretations
____ Literary Analysis: Audience ❑ Literary Analysis Transparencies, T1

Choices and Challenges

Writing Options
____ Firsthand Account
____ Essay on Leadership
____ Report to the President

Activities and Explorations
____ Miniseries Storyboard
____ Karankawa Speech
____ Informal Debate
____ Bar Graph

Inquiry and Research
____ Early Explorers

Art Connection
____ History Through Art

Copyright © McDougal Littell Inc.

Choices and Challenges (continued)

Vocabulary in Action
____ Context Clues

Author Activity
____ Just Like Fiction

Teaching Options (from Teacher's Edition)

Mini Lessons

Preteaching Vocabulary
____ Using Context Clues

Vocabulary Strategy
____ Applying Prefix and Root Word Meanings

❏ Vocabulary Transparencies and Copymasters, C27

Grammar
____ Simple Sentences: Subject, Predicate
____ Review: Parts of Speech

❏ Grammar Transparencies and Copymasters, C75
❏ Grammar Transparencies and Copymasters, C62

Speaking and Listening
____ Dramatic Reading and Retelling

Informal Assessment
____ Character Empathy

Assessment

____ Selection Quiz
____ Selection Test
____ Test Generator

❏ Unit One Resource Book: Selection Quiz, p. 35
❏ Formal Assessment: Selection Test, pp. 19–20

Homework Assignments

_____
_____
_____
_____

Other Teaching Materials

_____
_____
_____
_____

Copyright © McDougal Littell Inc.

from Of Plymouth Plantation

Core Objectives
- Understand and appreciate a historical chronicle
- Examine primary sources
- Summarize text by identifying main ideas and supporting details

Integrating Skills

Grammar
- Sentence Fragments
- Run-on Sentences

Vocabulary
- Using Context Clues
- Researching Word Origins

Preparing to Read
____ Connect to Your Life
____ Build Background
____ Vocabulary Preview: Using Context   ❏ Unit One Resource Book: Words to Know SkillBuilder, p. 39
      Clues
____ Focus Your Reading
      Literary Analysis: Primary Sources   ❏ Unit One Resource Book: Literary Analysis SkillBuilder, p. 38
      Active Reading: Summarizing   ❏ Unit One Resource Book: Active Reading SkillBuilder, p. 37

Teaching the Literature   ❏ PE pp. 81–90
____ Reading the Selection   ❏ Unit One Resource Book: Summary, p. 36

Thinking Through the Literature
____ Connect to the Literature
____ Think Critically   ❏ Reading and Critical Thinking Transparencies, T10, T19, T22
____ Extend Interpretations
____ Literary Analysis: Primary Sources   ❏ Literary Analysis Transparencies, T1, T2

Choices and Challenges

Writing Options
____ Squanto's Diary
____ Eyewitness Account
____ Interview Questions

Activities and Explorations
____ Pilgrim Memorial
____ Musical Soundtrack
____ Time Line

Inquiry and Research
____ The Voyage of the Pilgrims

Art Connection
____ Illustration of Plymouth Colony

Vocabulary in Action
____ Meaning Clues

Copyright © McDougal Littell Inc.

Choices and Challenges (continued)

Author Activity
____ Profiles in Courage

Teaching Options (from Teacher's Edition)

Mini Lessons

Preteaching Vocabulary
____ Using Context Clues

Vocabulary Strategy
____ Researching Word Origins   ❑ Vocabulary Transparencies and Copymasters, C22

Grammar
____ Sentence Fragments   ❑ Grammar Transparencies and Copymasters, C107
____ Run-on Sentences   ❑ Grammar Transparencies and Copymasters, C109

Speaking and Listening
____ Oral History

Viewing and Representing
Art Appreciation
____ *View of Plymouth, 1627* by Cal Sachs

Cross Curricular Link
Social Studies
____ Squanto

Informal Assessment
____ Parallel Account

Assessment
____ Selection Quiz   ❑ Unit One Resource Book: Selection Quiz, p. 40
____ Selection Test   ❑ Formal Assessment: Selection Test, pp. 21–22
____ Test Generator

Homework Assignments

_____
_____
_____
_____
_____

Other Teaching Materials

_____
_____
_____
_____
_____

Copyright © McDougal Littell Inc.

from The Interesting Narrative of the Life of Olaudah Equiano

Core Objectives
- Understand and appreciate a slave narrative
- Analyze details

Integrating Skills
Grammar
- Structure: Compound Sentences

Vocabulary
- Using Context Clues and Reference Materials

Preparing to Read
____ Connect to Your Life
____ Build Background
____ Vocabulary Preview: Using Context Clues and Reference Materials
____ Focus Your Reading
   Literary Analysis: Slave Narratives
   Active Reading: Analyzing Details

❏ Unit One Resource Book: Words to Know SkillBuilder, p. 44

❏ Unit One Resource Book: Literary Analysis SkillBuilder, p. 43
❏ Unit One Resource Book: Active Reading SkillBuilder, p. 42

Teaching the Literature
____ Reading the Selection

❏ PE pp. 93–99
❏ Unit One Resource Book: Summary, p. 41

Thinking Through the Literature
____ Connect to the Literature
____ Think Critically
____ Extend Interpretations
____ Literary Analysis: Slave Narratives

❏ Reading and Critical Thinking Transparencies, T10, T46

❏ Literary Analysis Transparencies, T1, T2

Choices and Challenges
Writing Options
____ Song of Freedom
____ Narrative Summary

Activities and Explorations
____ Museum Exhibit

Vocabulary in Action
____ Assessment Practice

Author Activity
____ Personal and Political

Copyright © McDougal Littell Inc.

from The Interesting Narrative of the Life of Olaudah Equiano

Teaching Options (from Teacher's Edition)

Mini Lessons

Preteaching Vocabulary

____ Using Context Clues and Reference Materials

Vocabulary Strategy

____ Using Context Clues and Reference Materials

Grammar

____ Structure: Compound Sentences ❏ Grammar Transparencies and Copymasters, C110

Viewing and Representing

Art Appreciation

____ *The Slave Ship* (detail) by Robert Riggs

Cross Curricular Link

History

____ Slavery

Informal Assessment

____ Open-Ended Test Questions

Assessment

____ Selection Quiz ❏ Unit One Resource Book: Selection Quiz, p. 45

____ Selection Test ❏ Formal Assessment: Selection Test, pp. 23–24

____ Test Generator

Homework Assignments	**Other Teaching Materials**
_____	_____
_____	_____
_____	_____
_____	_____
_____	_____

Copyright © McDougal Littell Inc.

from Blue Highways

Core Objectives
- Appreciate a travelogue
- Examine author's purpose
- Organize details

Integrating Skills

Grammar
- Complex Sentences
- Pronouns

Vocabulary
- Context Clues
- Prefixes, Suffixes, and Root Words

Preparing to Read
____ Comparing Literature
____ Build Background
____ Vocabulary Preview: Context Clues ☐ Unit One Resource Book: Words to Know SkillBuilder, p. 49
____ Focus Your Reading

Literary Analysis: Author's Purpose ☐ Unit One Resource Book: Literary Analysis SkillBuilder, p. 48

Active Reading: Organizing Details ☐ Unit One Resource Book: Active Reading SkillBuilder, p. 47

Teaching the Literature
____ Reading the Selection

☐ PE pp. 100–108
☐ Unit One Resource Book: Summary, p. 46

Thinking Through the Literature
____ Connect to the Literature
____ Think Critically ☐ Reading and Critical Thinking Transparencies, T19, T48, T55
____ Extend Interpretations
____ Literary Analysis: Author's Purpose ☐ Literary Analysis Transparencies, T16

Choices and Challenges

Writing Options
____ Hopi Dialogue
____ Personal Essay on Beliefs
____ Points of Comparison

Vocabulary in Action
____ Related Words

Copyright © McDougal Littell Inc.

Teaching Options (from Teacher's Edition)

Mini Lessons

Preteaching Vocabulary
____ Context Clues

Vocabulary Strategy
____ Prefixes, Suffixes, and Root Words

Grammar
____ Complex Sentences   ❑ Grammar Transparencies and Copymasters, C111
____ Pronouns   ❑ Grammar Transparencies and Copymasters, C125

Viewing and Representing
Art Appreciation
____ *Road Past the View* by Georgia O'Keefe

Cross Curricular Link

History
____ The Indian Citizenship Act of 1924

Informal Assessment
____ Distinguishing Between Fact and Nonfact

Assessment
____ Selection Quiz   ❑ Unit One Resource Book: Selection Quiz, p. 50
____ Selection Test   ❑ Formal Assessment: Selection Test, pp. 25–26
____ Test Generator

Homework Assignments	Other Teaching Materials

Copyright © McDougal Littell Inc.

My Sojourn in the Lands of My Ancestors

Core Objectives
- Understand and appreciate an autobiography
- Apply strategies for reading autobiography

Integrating Skills

Grammar
- Compound-Complex Sentences

Vocabulary
- Using Context Clues and Reference Materials

Preparing to Read

____ Comparing Literature

____ Build Background

____ Vocabulary Preview: Using Context Clues and Reference Materials   ❑ Unit One Resource Book: Words to Know SkillBuilder, p. 54

____ Focus Your Reading

Literary Analysis: Autobiography   ❑ Unit One Resource Book: Literary Analysis SkillBuilder, p. 53

Active Reading: Strategies for Reading Autobiography   ❑ Unit One Resource Book: Active Reading SkillBuilder, p. 52

Teaching the Literature

____ Reading the Selection

❑ PE pp. 109–117
❑ Unit One Resource Book: Summary, p. 51

Thinking Through the Literature

____ Connect to the Literature

____ Think Critically

____ Extend Interpretations

____ Literary Analysis: Autobiography

Choices and Challenges

Writing Options

____ Description of Place

____ Poetry of Experience

____ Points of Comparison

Vocabulary in Action

____ Meaning Clues

Copyright © McDougal Littell Inc.

My Sojourn in the Lands of My Ancestors

Teaching Options (from Teacher's Edition)

Mini Lessons

Preteaching Vocabulary
____ Using Context Clues and Reference Materials

Speaking and Listening
____ Poetry Reading

Grammar
____ Compound-Complex Sentences

Cross Curricular Link

History
____ Manhattan's African Burial Ground

Informal Assessment
____ Choosing the Best Summary

Assessment
____ Selection Quiz
____ Selection Test
____ Part Test
____ Test Generator

❑ Unit One Resource Book: Selection Quiz, p. 55
❑ Formal Assessment: Selection Test, pp. 27–28
❑ Formal Assessment: Unit One, Part 2 Test, pp. 29–30

Homework Assignments

_____

_____

_____

_____

_____

Other Teaching Materials

_____

_____

_____

_____

_____

Copyright © McDougal Littell Inc.

Eyewitness Report

Writing Prompt

Write an eyewitness report describing an event
that has personal or historical significance.

Preparing

____ Introduction

____ Basics in a Box

____ Using the Graphic

____ Analyzing a Student Model
"Far from the Land of Opportunity"

❏ Writing Transparencies and Copymasters, T11, T20, C25

❏ Unit One Resource Book: Student Models, pp. 62–67

Writing

____ **Prewriting**
Choosing a Subject
Planning the Eyewitness Report

❏ Unit One Resource Book: Prewriting, p. 57

____ **Drafting**
Organizing the Draft

❏ Unit One Resource Book: Drafting and Elaboration, p. 58

____ **Peer Review**
Ask Your Peer Reader

❏ Unit One Resource Book: Peer Response Guide, pp. 59–60

____ **Revising**
Elaborating with Sensory Details

❏ Unit One Resource Book: Revising, Editing, and Proofreading, p. 61
❏ Unit One Resource Book: Rubric for Evaluation, p. 68

____ **Editing and Proofreading**
Modifier Placement

____ **Reflecting**

Homework Assignments	**Other Teaching Materials**
_____	_____
_____	_____
_____	_____
_____	_____
_____	_____

Copyright © McDougal Littell Inc.

To My Dear and Loving Husband / Upon the Burning of Our House, July 10th, 1666

Pages 138–143

Core Objectives
- Understand and appreciate lyric poetry
- Appreciate author's use of meter
- Clarify meaning of archaic language

Integrating Skills

Grammar	Vocabulary
■ Auxiliary Verbs	■ Analogies

Preparing to Read
____ Connect to Your Life
____ Build Background
____ Focus Your Reading

Literary Analysis: Meter ❑ Unit Two Resource Book: Literary Analysis SkillBuilder, p. 5

Active Reading: Clarifying Meaning ❑ Unit Two Resource Book: Active Reading SkillBuilder, p. 4

Teaching the Literature
____ Reading the Selection ❑ PE pp. 138–143

Thinking Through the Literature
____ Connect to the Literature
____ Think Critically ❑ Reading and Critical Thinking Transparencies, T15, T26
____ Extend Interpretations
____ Literary Analysis: Meter ❑ Literary Analysis Transparencies, T11

Choices and Challenges

Writing Options
____ Lyric Poem
____ Personal Analogy

Activities and Explorations
____ Storyboard Illustrations
____ Musical Adaptation

Inquiry and Research
____ Puritan Women
____ Puritan Homes

Copyright © McDougal Littell Inc.

To My Dear and Loving Husband / Upon the Burning of Our House, July 10th, 1666

Teaching Options (from Teacher's Edition)

Mini Lessons

Vocabulary Strategy
____ Reading and Understanding Analogies ❑ Vocabulary Transparencies and Copymasters, C24

Grammar
____ Auxiliary Verbs ❑ Grammar Transparencies and Copymasters, C67

Informal Assessment
____ Journal Entry

Assessment
____ Selection Test ❑ Formal Assessment: Selection Test, pp. 31–32
____ Test Generator

Homework Assignments

_____

_____

_____

_____

Other Teaching Materials

_____

_____

_____

_____

Copyright © McDougal Littell Inc.

The Examination of Sarah Good

Core Objectives
- Understand and appreciate a court transcript
- Detect bias in a speaker's language

Integrating Skills

Grammar
- Overuse of the Verb *To Be*

Vocabulary
- Idioms

Preparing to Read
____ Connect to Your Life
____ Build Background
____ Focus Your Reading
Literary Analysis: Transcript
Active Reading: Detecting Bias
Active Reading: Distinguishing Fact from Opinion

❑ Unit Two Resource Book: Literary Analysis SkillBuilder, p. 8
❑ Unit Two Resource Book: Active Reading SkillBuilder, p. 7

Teaching the Literature
____ Reading the Selection

❑ PE pp. 144–149
❑ Unit Two Resource Book: Summary, p. 6

Thinking Through the Literature
____ Connect to the Literature
____ Think Critically
____ Extend Interpretations
____ Literary Analysis: Transcript

❑ Reading and Critical Thinking Transparencies, T22

Choices and Challenges

Writing Options
____ Courtroom Drama
____ Plea for Mercy
____ Explanation of Motives

Activities and Explorations
____ Courtroom Sketches
____ Media Coverage
____ Legal Discussion

Inquiry and Research
____ Salem Witch Trials
____ Salem Memorials

Art Connection
____ Mental Picture

Copyright © McDougal Littell Inc.

The Examination of Sarah Good

Teaching Options (from Teacher's Edition)

Mini Lessons

Vocabulary Strategy
____ Using Context to Determine the Meaning of Idioms

❑ Vocabulary Transparencies and Copymasters, C25

Grammar
____ Overuse of the Verb *To Be*

❑ Grammar Transparencies and Copymasters, C163

Informal Assessment
____ Understanding Multiple-Meaning Words

Assessment
____ Selection Quiz

____ Selection Test

____ Test Generator

❑ Unit Two Resource Book: Selection Quiz, p. 9

❑ Formal Assessment: Selection Test, pp. 33–34

Homework Assignments

_____

_____

_____

_____

_____

Other Teaching Materials

_____

_____

_____

_____

_____

Copyright © McDougal Littell Inc.

from Sinners in the Hands of an Angry God   Pages 152–160

Core Objectives
- Analyze an 18th-century sermon
- Appreciate author's use of persuasive writing
- Analyze emotional language

Integrating Skills

Grammar
- Subject-Verb Agreement

Vocabulary
- Context Clues
- Connotation

Preparing to Read
____ Connect to Your Life
____ Build Background
____ Vocabulary Preview: Using Context Clues   ❏ Unit Two Resource Book: Words to Know SkillBuilder, p. 13
____ Focus Your Reading
     Literary Analysis: Persuasive Writing   ❏ Unit Two Resource Book: Literary Analysis SkillBuilder, p. 12
     Active Reading: Analyzing Emotional Language   ❏ Unit Two Resource Book: Active Reading SkillBuilder, p. 11

Teaching the Literature
     ❏ PE pp. 152–160
____ Reading the Selection   ❏ Unit Two Resource Book: Summary, p. 10

Thinking Through the Literature
____ Connect to the Literature
____ Think Critically   ❏ Reading and Critical Thinking Transparencies, T15, T18
____ Extend Interpretations
____ Literary Analysis: Persuasive Writing   ❏ Literary Analysis Transparencies, T9

Choices and Challenges

Writing Options
____ Letter of Opinion
____ Vivid Comparison
____ Public Service Announcement

Activities and Explorations
____ Live Performance
____ Jacket Cover

Inquiry and Research
____ Inspirational Speakers
____ Artistic Visions

Vocabulary in Action
____ Assessment Practice

Author Activity
____ A Vision of Terror and Beauty

Copyright © McDougal Littell Inc.

from Sinners in the Hands of an Angry God

Teaching Options (from Teacher's Edition)

Mini Lessons

Preteaching Vocabulary
____ Using Context Clues

Vocabulary Strategy
____ Interpreting the Connotative Power of Words   ❑ Vocabulary Transparencies and Copymasters, C26

Grammar
____ Subject-Verb Agreement   ❑ Grammar Transparencies and Copymasters, C123

Viewing and Representing
Art Appreciation
____ *Un quadro di fuochi preziosi [A painting of precious fires]* by Enzo Cucchi

Cross Curricular Link

History
____ Puritan Intolerance

Informal Assessment
____ Choosing the Best Summary

Assessment
____ Selection Quiz   ❑ Unit Two Resource Book: Selection Quiz, p. 14
____ Selection Test   ❑ Formal Assessment: Selection Test, pp. 35–36
____ Test Generator

Homework Assignments
_____
_____
_____
_____

Other Teaching Materials
_____
_____
_____
_____

Copyright © McDougal Littell Inc.

The Crucible, Act One

Core Objectives

- Understand and appreciate a drama
- Understand author's use of stage directions
- Use a graphic organizer to keep track of details in a play

Integrating Skills

Grammar

- Interjections
- Regular and Irregular Verbs
- Principal Parts of Verbs
- Perfect Tenses

Vocabulary

- Using Reference Materials
- Prefixes and Root Words
- Context Clues
- Multiple-Meaning Words
- Word Origins

Preparing to Read

____ Comparing Literature

____ Build Background

____ Vocabulary Preview: Using Reference Materials

❑ Unit Two Resource Book: Words to Know SkillBuilder, p. 18, p. 23, p. 28, p. 33

____ Focus Your Reading
Literary Analysis: Stage Directions
Active Reading: Using a Graphic Organizer

❑ Unit Two Resource Book: Literary Analysis SkillBuilder, p. 17, p. 22, p. 27, p. 32

❑ Unit Two Resource Book: Active Reading SkillBuilder, p. 16, p. 21, p. 26, p. 31

Teaching the Literature

____ Reading the Selection

❑ PE pp. 163–190

❑ Unit Two Resource Book: Summary, p. 15

Thinking Through the Literature

____ Connect to the Literature

____ Think Critically

____ Extend Interpretations

❑ Reading and Critical Thinking Transparencies, T6, T15, T52

____ Literary Analysis: Stage Directions

❑ Literary Analysis Transparencies, T3, T4, T5

Copyright © McDougal Littell Inc.

The Crucible, Act One

Teaching Options (from Teacher's Edition)

Mini Lessons

Preteaching Vocabulary
____ Using Reference Materials

Vocabulary Strategy
____ Applying Meanings of Prefixes and Root Words

❑ Vocabulary Transparencies and Copymasters, C27

Grammar
____ Interjections
____ Regular and Irregular Verbs

❑ Grammar Transparencies and Copymasters, C72
❑ Grammar Transparencies and Copymasters, C113

Viewing and Representing
____ Photograph

Cross Curricular Link

History
____ Barbados

Informal Assessment

____ Recognizing Facts and Details
____ Making Inferences and Drawing Conclusions
____ Alternative Ending

Assessment

____ Selection Quiz
____ Selection Test
____ Test Generator

❑ Unit Two Resource Book: Selection Quiz, p. 19
❑ Formal Assessment: Selection Test, pp. 37–38

Homework Assignments

_____
_____
_____
_____
_____

Other Teaching Materials

_____
_____
_____
_____
_____

Copyright © McDougal Littell Inc.

Name _____ Date _____

The Crucible, Act Two

Core Objectives
See page 29.

Integrating Skills

Grammar
- Principal Parts of Verbs

Vocabulary
- Using Context Clues
- Applying Prefixes and Root Words

Teaching the Literature
____ Reading the Selection

❑ PE pp. 191–206
❑ Unit Two Resource Book: Summary, p. 20

Thinking Through the Literature
____ Connect to the Literature
____ Think Critically
____ Extend Interpretations
____ Literary Analysis: Dialogue

❑ Reading and Critical Thinking Transparencies, T6, T15, T52

❑ Literary Analysis Transparencies, T3, T4, T5

Teaching Options (from Teacher's Edition)

Mini Lessons

Vocabulary Strategy
____ Using Context Clues
____ Applying Prefixes and Root Words

❑ Vocabulary Transparencies and Copymasters, C27

Grammar
____ Principal Parts of Verbs

❑ Grammar Transparencies and Copymasters, C114

Viewing and Representing
____ Photograph

Cross Curricular Link

History
____ McCarthy Hearings

Informal Assessment
____ Arranging Events in Sequential Order
____ Perceiving Cause and Effect Relationships

Copyright © McDougal Littell Inc.

Assessment

____ Selection Quiz

____ Selection Test

____ Test Generator

❑ Unit Two Resource Book: Selection Quiz, p. 24

❑ Formal Assessment: Selection Test, pp. 39–40

Homework Assignments

_____

_____

_____

_____

_____

Other Teaching Materials

_____

_____

_____

_____

_____

Copyright © McDougal Littell Inc.

The Crucible, Act Three

Core Objectives
See page 29.

Integrating Skills

Grammar
- Perfect Tenses

Vocabulary
- Using Context Clues
- Understanding Multiple-
  Meaning Words

Teaching the Literature
____ Reading the Selection

❑ PE pp. 207–228
❑ Unit Two Resource Book: Summary, p. 25

Thinking Through the Literature
____ Connect to the Literature
____ Think Critically
____ Extend Interpretations
____ Literary Analysis: Foil

❑ Reading and Critical Thinking Transparencies, T6, T15, T52

❑ Literary Analysis Transparencies, T3, T4, T5

Teaching Options (from Teacher's Edition)

Mini Lessons

Vocabulary Strategy
____ Using Context Clues
____ Understanding Multiple-Meaning Words

Grammar
____ Perfect Tenses

❑ Grammar Transparencies and Copymasters, C115

Speaking and Listening
____ Role-Playing

Cross Curricular Links

History
____ Witchcraft Trials

Logic
____ Inductive and Deductive Reasoning

Psychology
____ Hysteria

Informal Assessment
____ Court Reporter
____ Predicting Probable Future Actions
____ Describing Character

Copyright © McDougal Littell Inc.

Assessment

____ Selection Quiz

____ Selection Test

____ Test Generator

❑ Unit Two Resource Book: Selection Quiz, p. 29

❑ Formal Assessment: Selection Test, pp. 41–42

Homework Assignments

_____

_____

_____

_____

_____

Other Teaching Materials

_____

_____

_____

_____

_____

Copyright © McDougal Littell Inc.

The Crucible, Act Four

Core Objectives
See page 29.

Integrating Skills
Vocabulary
- Using Context Clues
- Researching Word Origins

Teaching the Literature
___ Reading the Selection

☐ PE pp. 229–245
☐ Unit Two Resource Book: Summary, p. 30

Thinking Through the Literature
___ Connect to the Literature
___ Think Critically
___ Extend Interpretations
___ Literary Analysis: Plot and Conflict

☐ Reading and Critical Thinking Transparencies, T6, T15, T52

☐ Literary Analysis Transparencies, T3, T4, T5

Choices and Challenges
Writing Options
___ Points of Comparison
___ Missing Scene
___ Editorial on Hysteria
___ Capsule Review

Activities and Explorations
___ Historical Fashions
___ Set Design
___ Dramatic Reading
___ Salem Game Show

Inquiry and Research
___ History vs. Drama
___ McCarthyism

Vocabulary in Action
___ Context Clues
___ Assessment Practice

Copyright © McDougal Littell Inc.

The Crucible, Act Four

Teaching Options (from Teacher's Edition)

Mini Lessons

Vocabulary Strategy
____ Using Context Clues
____ Researching Word Origins

Speaking and Listening
____ Staging a Mock Trial
____ Performing the Climactic Scene

Viewing and Representing
____ Darkness and Light

Cross Curricular Link

Workplace
____ Communicating

Informal Assessment
____ Making Inferences
____ Alternative Ending

Assessment
____ Selection Quiz
____ Selection Test
____ Part Test

❑ Unit Two Resource Book: Selection Quiz, p. 34
❑ Formal Assessment: Selection Test, pp. 43–44
❑ Formal Assessment: Unit Two: Part 1 Test, pp. 45–46

Homework Assignments

_____

_____

_____

_____

_____

Other Teaching Materials

_____

_____

_____

_____

_____

Copyright © McDougal Littell Inc.

Critical Review

Writing Prompt

Write a review of a piece of literature or a film
you feel strongly about. You will establish
evaluation criteria and express your opinion
of the piece.

Preparing

___ Introduction
___ Basics in a Box
___ Using the Graphic

❑ Writing Transparencies and Copymasters, T11, T20, C26

___ Analyzing a Professional Model
"Movie Review of *The Crucible*"

❑ Unit Two Resource Book: Student Models, pp. 41–46

Writing

___ **Prewriting**
Choosing a Subject
Planning the Critical Review

❑ Unit Two Resource Book: Prewriting, p. 36

___ **Drafting**
Organizing the Draft

❑ Unit Two Resource Book: Drafting and Elaboration, p. 37

___ **Peer Review**
Ask Your Peer Reader

❑ Unit Two Resource Book: Peer Response Guide, pp. 38–39

___ **Revising**
Avoiding Circular Reasoning

❑ Unit Two Resource Book: Revising, Editing, and Proofreading, p. 40
❑ Unit Two Resource Book: Rubric for Evaluation, p. 47

___ **Editing and Proofreading**
Eliminating Qualifiers

___ **Reflecting**

Homework Assignments

_____
_____
_____
_____
_____

Other Teaching Materials

_____
_____
_____
_____
_____

Copyright © McDougal Littell Inc.

Speech in the Virginia Convention

Core Objectives
- Understand a persuasive speech
- Appreciate use of allusion
- Analyze the use of rhetorical questions and persuasion

Integrating Skills

Grammar
- Perfect Tenses

Vocabulary
- Context Clues

Preparing to Read
____ Connect to Your Life
____ Build Background
____ Vocabulary Preview: Using Context Clues   ❑ Unit Two Resource Book: Words to Know SkillBuilder, p. 53
____ Focus Your Reading
     Literary Analysis: Allusion   ❑ Unit Two Resource Book: Literary Analysis SkillBuilder, p. 52
     Active Reading: Rhetorical Questions and   ❑ Unit Two Resource Book: Active Reading SkillBuilder, p. 51
      Persuasion

Teaching the Literature
                                         ❑ PE pp. 262–269
____ Reading the Selection   ❑ Unit Two Resource Book: Summary, p. 50

Thinking Through the Literature
____ Connect to the Literature
____ Think Critically   ❑ Reading and Critical Thinking Transparencies, T20, T21
____ Extend Interpretations
____ Literary Analysis: Allusion   ❑ Literary Analysis Transparencies, T9

Choices and Challenges

Writing Options
____ Newspaper Report
____ Character Sketch
____ Rebuttal Speech

Activities and Explorations
____ Political Advertisement
____ Liberty Poster
____ Dramatic Reading
____ Independence Discussion

Art Connection

Inquiry and Research
____ Countdown to Revolution

Vocabulary in Action
____ Classifying Words

Copyright © McDougal Littell Inc.

Speech in the Virginia Convention

Teaching Options (from Teacher's Edition)

Mini Lessons

Preteaching Vocabulary
____ Context Clues

Grammar
____ Perfect Tenses

❑ Grammar Transparencies and Copymasters, C116

Viewing and Representing
Art Appreciation
____ *Patrick Henry Before the Virginia House of Burgesses* by Peter F. Rothermel

Cross Curricular Link

American History
____ Patrick Henry

Informal Assessment
____ Understanding Multiple Word Meanings

Assessment
____ Selection Quiz
____ Selection Test
____ Test Generator

❑ Unit Two Resource Book: Selection Quiz, p. 54
❑ Formal Assessment: Selection Test, pp. 47–48

Homework Assignments

_____
_____
_____
_____

Other Teaching Materials

_____
_____
_____
_____

Copyright © McDougal Littell Inc.

The Declaration of Independence

Core Objectives
- Understand a document of critical importance in U.S. history
- Recognize examples of parallelism
- Construct meaning by paraphrasing difficult passages

Integrating Skills

Grammar
- Capitalization
- Verbs: Avoiding Shifts

Vocabulary
- Using Context Clues
- Using a Thesaurus

Preparing to Read
____ Connect to Your Life
____ Build Background
____ Vocabulary Preview   ❑ Unit Two Resource Book: Words to Know SkillBuilder, p. 58
____ Focus Your Reading
     Literary Analysis: Parallelism   ❑ Unit Two Resource Book: Literary Analysis SkillBuilder, p. 57
     Active Reading: Paraphrasing   ❑ Unit Two Resource Book: Active Reading SkillBuilder, p. 56

Teaching the Literature
     ❑ PE pp. 270–281
____ Reading the Selection   ❑ Unit Two Resource Book: Summary, p. 55

Thinking Through the Literature
____ Connect to the Literature
____ Think Critically   ❑ Reading and Critical Thinking Transparencies, T41
____ Extend Interpretations
____ Literary Analysis: Parallelism   ❑ Literary Analysis Transparencies, T10

Choices and Challenges

Writing Options
____ Modern Paraphrase
____ Teenager's Declaration
____ Personal Response

Activities and Explorations
____ Taking Slides
____ First Draft Blues
____ Colonial Cartoon

Vocabulary in Action
Context Clues
____

Copyright © McDougal Littell Inc.

The Declaration of Independence

Teaching Options (from Teacher's Edition)

Mini Lessons

Preteaching Vocabulary
____ Using Context Clues

Vocabulary Strategy
____ Using a Thesaurus to Determine Synonyms

❑ Vocabulary Transparencies and Copymasters, C31

Grammar
____ Capitalization
____ Verbs: Avoiding Shifts in Tense, Mood, and Voice

❑ Grammar Transparencies and Copymasters, C144
❑ Grammar Transparencies and Copymasters, C120

Viewing and Representing
Art Appreciation
____ *Signing the Declaration of Independence* by John Trumbull

Cross Curricular Links

History
____ The Age of Enlightenment
____ Legal Rights of Women in 1776

Informal Assessment
____ Making Inferences and Drawing Conclusions
____ Retelling

Assessment
____ Selection Quiz
____ Selection Test
____ Test Generator

❑ Unit Two Resource Book: Selection Quiz, p. 59
❑ Formal Assessment: Selection Test, pp. 49–50

Homework Assignments

_____
_____
_____
_____
_____

Other Teaching Materials

_____
_____
_____
_____
_____

Copyright © McDougal Littell Inc.

Letter to the Rev. Samson Occom /
Letter to John Adams

Core Objectives
- Understand and appreciate literary letters
- Appreciate author's use of figurative language
- Use strategies for reading literary letters

Integrating Skills

Grammar
- Using Correct
  Verb Forms

Vocabulary
- Using Context Clues

Preparing to Read
____ Connect to Your Life
____ Build Background
____ Vocabulary Preview: Using Context Clues   ❑ Unit Two Resource Book: Words to Know SkillBuilder, p. 64
____ Focus Your Reading
        Literary Analysis: Figurative Language   ❑ Unit Two Resource Book: Literary Analysis SkillBuilder, p. 63
        Active Reading: Literary Letters   ❑ Unit Two Resource Book: Active Reading SkillBuilder, p. 62

Teaching the Literature
                                                         ❑ PE pp. 282–288
____ Reading the Selection   ❑ Unit Two Resource Book: Summary, p. 60

Thinking Through the Literature
____ Connect to the Literature
____ Think Critically   ❑ Reading and Critical Thinking Transparencies, T7
____ Extend Interpretations
____ Literary Analysis: Figurative Language

Choices and Challenges

Writing Options
____ Literary Letter

Activities and Explorations
____ Talk Show

Vocabulary in Action
____ Assessment Practice

Copyright © McDougal Littell Inc.

Letter to the Rev. Samson Occom /
Letter to John Adams

Teaching Options (from Teacher's Edition)

Mini Lessons

Preteaching Vocabulary
____ Using Context Clues

Grammar
____ Using Correct Verb Forms   ❏ Grammar Transparencies and Copymasters, C117

Viewing and Representing
Art Appreciation
____ *The Edenton Ladies Tea Party*

____ *Informal Assessment*

Assessment

____ Selection Quiz   ❏ Unit Two Resource Book: Selection Quiz, p. 65
____ Selection Test   ❏ Formal Assessment: Selection Test, pp. 51–52
____ Test Generator

Homework Assignments

_____
_____
_____
_____
_____

Other Teaching Materials

_____
_____
_____
_____

Copyright © McDougal Littell Inc.

What Is an American?

Core Objectives
- Understand and appreciate an essay
- Understand and appreciate use of theme
- Analyze contrast in an essay

Integrating Skills
Grammar
- Using Verbs: Voice and Mood

Vocabulary
- Using Context Clues

Preparing to Read
____ Connect to Your Life
____ Build Background
____ Vocabulary Preview: Using Context Clues   ❑ Unit Two Resource Book: Words to Know SkillBuilder, p. 69
____ Focus Your Reading
    Literary Analysis: Theme   ❑ Unit Two Resource Book: Literary Analysis SkillBuilder, p. 68
    Active Reading: Analyzing Contrast   ❑ Unit Two Resource Book: Active Reading SkillBuilder, p. 67

Teaching the Literature
❑ PE pp. 289–294
____ Reading the Selection   ❑ Unit One Resource Book: Summary, p. 66

Thinking Through the Literature
____ Connect to the Literature
____ Think Critically   ❑ Reading and Critical Thinking Transparencies, T15, T50
____ Extend Interpretations
____ Literary Analysis: Theme   ❑ Literary Analysis Transparencies, T22

Choices and Challenges
Writing Options
____ Draft of Article
____ Local Definition

Vocabulary in Action
____ Context Clues

Copyright © McDougal Littell Inc.

What Is an American?

Teaching Options (from Teacher's Edition)

Mini Lessons

Preteaching Vocabulary
____ Using Context Clues

Grammar
____ Using Verbs: Voice and Mood   ❑ Grammar Transparencies and Copymasters, C119

Viewing and Representing
Art Appreciation
____ *Van Bergen Overmantel*
attributed to John Heaten

Informal Assessment
____ Perceiving Cause and Effect

Assessment

____ Selection Quiz   ❑ Unit Two Resource Book: Selection Quiz, p. 70
____ Selection Test   ❑ Formal Assessment: Selection Test, p. 53
____ Test Generator

Homework Assignments

_____

_____

_____

_____

_____

Other Teaching Materials

_____

_____

_____

_____

Copyright © McDougal Littell Inc.

Lecture to a Missionary

Core Objectives
- Understand and appreciate a speech
- Appreciate author's use of tone
- Draw conclusions about tone

Integrating Skills

Grammar
- Commonly Confused Verbs

Vocabulary
- Understanding Figurative Language

Preparing to Read
____ Connect to Your Life
____ Build Background
____ Focus Your Reading
     Literary Analysis: Tone   ❑ Unit Two Resource Book: Literary Analysis SkillBuilder, p. 73
     Active Reading: Drawing Conclusions About Tone ❑ Unit Two Resource Book: Active Reading SkillBuilder, p. 72

Teaching the Literature
____ Reading the Selection   ❑ PE pp. 295–299
                        ❑ Unit Two Resource Book: Summary, p. 71

Thinking Through the Literature
____ Connect to the Literature
____ Think Critically   ❑ Reading and Critical Thinking Transparencies, T4
____ Extend Interpretations
____ Literary Analysis: Tone   ❑ Literary Analysis Transparencies, T19

Choices and Challenges
Writing Options
____ Mediator's Recommendations
____ Cran's Response
____ Tolerance Pamphlet

Activities and Explorations
____ Re-created Speech
____ Mural of Seneca History

Copyright © McDougal Littell Inc.

Lecture to a Missionary

Teaching Options (from Teacher's Edition)

Mini Lessons

Vocabulary Strategy
____ Understanding Figurative Language   ❑ Vocabulary Transparencies and Copymasters, C32

Grammar
____ Commonly Confused Verbs   ❑ Grammar Transparencies and Copymasters, C122

Speaking and Listening
____ Speech

Assessment
____ Selection Quiz   ❑ Unit Two Resource Book: Selection Quiz, p. 74
____ Selection Test   ❑ Formal Assessment: Selection Test, p. 55
____ Test Generator

Homework Assignments

_____

_____

_____

_____

Other Teaching Materials

_____

_____

_____

_____

Copyright © McDougal Littell Inc.

from Stride Toward Freedom /
Necessary to Protect Ourselves

Core Objectives
- Understand and appreciate an excerpt and a transcript of an interview
- Understand the historical context of a literary work
- Analyze the structure of arguments

Integrating Skills

Grammar
- Past Perfect Tense

Vocabulary
- Using Context Clues
- Connotations and Idioms

Preparing to Read
____ Connect to Your Life
____ Build Background
____ Vocabulary Preview: Using Context Clues   ❑ Unit Two Resource Book: Words to Know SkillBuilder, p. 79
____ Focus Your Reading
        Literary Analysis: Historical Context   ❑ Unit Two Resource Book: Literary Analysis SkillBuilder, p. 78
        Active Reading: Analyzing the Structure   ❑ Unit Two Resource Book: Active Reading SkillBuilder, p. 77
        of Arguments

Teaching the Literature   ❑ PE pp. 300–308
____ Reading the Selection   ❑ Unit Two Resource Book: Summary, p. 76

Thinking Through the Literature
____ Connect to the Literature
____ Think Critically   ❑ Reading and Critical Thinking Transparencies, T17, T21, T23
____ Extend Interpretations
____ Literary Analysis: Historical Context   ❑ Literary Analysis Transparencies, T16

Choices and Challenges
Writing Options
____ Points of Comparison

Vocabulary in Action
____ Word Knowledge

Copyright © McDougal Littell Inc.

from Stride Toward Freedom / Necessary to Protect Ourselves

Teaching Options (from Teacher's Edition)

Mini Lessons

Preteaching Vocabulary
____ Using Context Clues

Vocabulary Strategy
____ Understanding Connotations and Idioms   ❑ Vocabulary Transparencies and Copymasters, C36

Grammar
____ Past Perfect Tense   ❑ Grammar Transparencies and Copymasters, C116

Speaking and Listening
____ Debate

Informal Assessment
____ Identifying the Main Idea

Assessment
____ Selection Quiz   ❑ Unit Two Resource Book: Selection Quiz, p. 80
____ Selection Test   ❑ Formal Assessment: Selection Test, pp. 57–58
____ Test Generator

Homework Assignments
_____
_____
_____
_____
_____

Other Teaching Materials
_____
_____
_____
_____
_____

Copyright © McDougal-Littell Inc.

I Am Joaquin / Yo Soy Joaquín

Core Objectives
- Understand and appreciate an epic poem
- Use strategies for reading epic poetry

Integrating Skills

Grammar
- Problems in Using Verb Tenses

Vocabulary
- Researching Word Origins

Preparing to Read
____ Comparing Literature
____ Connect to Your Life
____ Build Background
____ Focus Your Reading
Literary Analysis: Epic Poem   ❑ Unit Two Resource Book: Literary Analysis SkillBuilder, p. 82
Active Reading: Strategies for Reading Epic Poetry   ❑ Unit Two Resource Book: Active Reading SkillBuilder, p. 81

Teaching the Literature
____ Reading the Selection   ❑ PE pp. 309–317

Thinking Through the Literature
____ Connect to the Literature
____ Think Critically   ❑ Reading and Critical Thinking Transparencies, T16, T55
____ Extend Interpretations
____ Literary Analysis: Epic Poem   ❑ Literary Analysis Transparencies, T16

Choices and Challenges

Writing Options
____ Book Review
____ Points of Comparison

Activities and Explorations
____ Choral Reading
____ Language Study

Author Activity
____ Rodolfo Gonzales

Copyright © McDougal Littell Inc.

I Am Joaquin / Yo Soy Joaquín

Teaching Options (from Teacher's Edition)

Mini Lessons

Vocabulary Strategy
____ Researching Word Origins ❑ Vocabulary Transparencies and Copymasters, C43

Speaking and Listening
____ Poetry Reading Workshop

Grammar
____ Problems in Using Verb Tenses ❑ Grammar Transparencies and Copymasters, T46, C121

Viewing and Representing
Art Appreciation
____ *The Farmworkers of Guadalupe*
by Judith F. Baca

Cross Curricular Link

History
____ Cesar Chavez

Informal Assessment
____ Defining Character

Assessment

____ Selection Test ❑ Formal Assessment: Selection Test, pp. 59–60
____ Part Test ❑ Formal Assessment: Unit Two, Part 2, pp. 61–62
____ Test Generator

Homework Assignments

_____
_____
_____
_____

Other Teaching Materials

_____
_____
_____
_____

Copyright © McDougal Littell Inc.

Persuasive Essay

Writing Prompt

Write a persuasive essay about
an issue that concerns you.

Preparing

____ Introduction
____ Basics in a Box
____ Using the Graphic

❑ Writing Transparencies and Copymasters, T11, T20, C27

____ Analyzing a Student Model
"Security Cameras in Schools"

❑ Unit Two Resource Book: Student Models, pp. 89–94

Writing

____ **Prewriting**
Choosing an Issue
Planning Your Persuasive Essay

❑ Unit Two Resource Book: Prewriting, p. 84

____ **Drafting**
Organizing the Draft

❑ Unit Two Resource Book: Drafting and Elaboration, p. 85

____ **Peer Review**
Ask Your Peer Reader

❑ Unit Two Resource Book: Peer Response Guide, pp. 86–87

____ **Revising**
Supporting Personal Opinions with Facts

❑ Unit Two Resource Book: Revising, Editing, and Proofreading, p. 88
❑ Unit Two Resource Book: Rubric for Evaluation, p. 95

____ **Editing and Proofreading**
Pronoun-Antecedent Agreement

____ **Reflecting**

Homework Assignments

_____

_____

_____

_____

_____

Other Teaching Materials

_____

_____

_____

_____

_____

Copyright © McDougal Littell Inc.

A Psalm of Life

Core Objectives
- Understand and appreciate a classic lyric poem
- Examine stanza and rhyme scheme
- Use strategies for reading traditional poetry

Integrating Skills

Grammar
- Noun Phrases

Vocabulary
- Homonyms

Preparing to Read

___ Connect to Your Life
___ Build Background
___ Focus Your Reading
    Literary Analysis: Stanza and Rhyme Scheme   ❏ Unit Three Resource Book: Literary Analysis SkillBuilder, p. 5
    Active Reading: Strategies for   ❏ Unit Three Resource Book: Active Reading SkillBuilder, p. 4
      Reading Traditional Poetry

Teaching the Literature

___ Reading the Selection   ❏ PE pp. 344–348

Thinking Through the Literature

___ Connect to the Literature
___ Think Critically   ❏ Reading and Critical Thinking Transparencies, T51
___ Extend Interpretations
___ Literary Analysis: Stanza and Rhyme Scheme   ❏ Literary Analysis Transparencies, T11

Choices and Challenges

Writing Options
___ Personal Response
___ Longfellow Parody

Activities and Explorations
___ Photo Collage
___ Bumper Sticker

___ **Author Activity**

Copyright © McDougal Littell Inc.

Teaching Options (from Teacher's Edition)

Mini Lessons

Vocabulary Strategy

___ Homonyms

❏ Vocabulary Transparencies and Copymasters, C35

Grammar

___ Noun Phrases

❏ Grammar Transparencies and Copymasters, C80

Viewing and Representing

Art Appreciation

___ *En Mer [At Sea]* by Max Bohm

Assessment

___ Selection Test

___ Test Generator

❏ Formal Assessment: Selection Test, pp. 63–64

Homework Assignments

_____

_____

_____

_____

_____

Other Teaching Materials

_____

_____

_____

_____

_____

Copyright © McDougal Littell Inc.

The Devil and Tom Walker

Core Objectives
- Understand and appreciate a short story
- Identify imagery in a short story
- Visualize the characters, setting, and events in a short story

Integrating Skills

Grammar
- Verbal Phrases: Infinitives, Gerunds, and Participles
- Using Modifiers Correctly

Vocabulary
- Using Context Clues
- Idioms
- Word Origins

Preparing to Read
____ Connect to Your Life
____ Build Background
____ Vocabulary Preview: Using Context Clues ❑ Unit Three Resource Book: Words to Know SkillBuilder, p. 9
____ Focus Your Reading
Literary Analysis: Imagery ❑ Unit Three Resource Book: Literary Analysis SkillBuilder, p. 8
Active Reading: Visualizing ❑ Unit Three Resource Book: Active Reading SkillBuilder, p. 7

Teaching the Literature
❑ PE pp. 349–362
____ Reading the Selection ❑ Unit Three Resource Book: Summary, p. 6

Thinking Through the Literature
____ Connect to the Literature
____ Think Critically ❑ Reading and Critical Thinking Transparencies, T8
____ Extend Interpretations
____ Literary Analysis: Imagery ❑ Literary Analysis Transparencies, T18, T24

Choices and Challenges

Writing Options
____ Reflective Essay on Wealth
____ Fitting Proverbs
____ Updated Faust Legend

Activities and Explorations
____ Board Game

Vocabulary in Action
____ Assessment Practice
____ Meaning Clues

Author Activity
____ Tales Compared

Copyright © McDougal Littell Inc.

The Devil and Tom Walker

Teaching Options (from Teacher's Edition)

Mini Lessons

Preteaching Vocabulary
____ Using Context Clues

Vocabulary Strategy
____ Idioms   ❑ Vocabulary Transparencies and Copymasters, C36
____ Word Origins

Grammar
____ Verbal Phrases: Infinitives, Gerunds, and Participles
____ Using Modifiers Correctly   ❑ Grammar Transparencies and Copymasters, C127

Cross Curricular Links

Multicultural
____ Folklore

Economics
____ Usury

Informal Assessment
____ Story Map
____ Recognize Facts and Details

Assessment
____ Selection Quiz   ❑ Unit Three Resource Book: Selection Quiz, p. 10
____ Selection Test   ❑ Formal Assessment: Selection Test, pp. 65–66
____ Test Generator

Homework Assignments

_____
_____
_____
_____
_____

Other Teaching Materials

_____
_____
_____
_____
_____

Copyright © McDougal Littell Inc.

Core Objectives
- Understand and appreciate a transcendentalist essay
- Appreciate author's use of aphorisms
- Use summarizing to understand an essay

Integrating Skills

Grammar
- Adjective and Adverb Phrases

Vocabulary
- Context Clues

Preparing to Read
____ Connect to Your Life
____ Build Background
____ Vocabulary Preview: Using Context Clues   ❑ Unit Three Resource Book: Words to Know SkillBuilder, p. 14
____ Focus Your Reading
Literary Analysis: Aphorism   ❑ Unit Three Resource Book: Literary Analysis SkillBuilder, p. 13
Active Reading: Summarizing   ❑ Unit Three Resource Book: Active Reading SkillBuilder, p. 12

Teaching the Literature
                                                   ❑ PE pp. 363–368
____ Reading the Selection   ❑ Unit Three Resource Book: Summary, p. 11

Thinking Through the Literature
____ Connect to the Literature
____ Think Critically   ❑ Reading and Critical Thinking Transparencies, T10
____ Extend Interpretations
____ Literary Analysis: Aphorism   ❑ Literary Analysis Transparencies, T8

Choices and Challenges

Writing Options
____ Personal Essay
____ Update of Emerson

Inquiry and Research
____ History

Vocabulary in Action
____ Meaning Clues

____ **Author Activity**

Copyright © McDougal Littell Inc.

from Self-Reliance

Teaching Options (from Teacher's Edition)

Mini Lessons

Preteaching Vocabulary
____ Using Context Clues

Grammar
____ Modifiers: Adjective and Adverb
Phrases

❏ Grammar Transparencies and Copymasters, C82

Viewing and Representing
Art Appreciation
____ *Kindred Spirits* by Asher B. Durand

Informal Assessment

____ Recognize the Author's Point of View
and Purpose

Assessment

____ Selection Quiz
____ Selection Test
____ Test Generator

❏ Unit Three Resource Book: Selection Quiz, p. 15
❏ Formal Assessment: Selection Test, pp. 67–68

Homework Assignments

_____

_____

_____

_____

_____

Other Teaching Materials

_____

_____

_____

_____

Copyright © McDougal Littell Inc.

Core Objectives
- Understand and appreciate a persuasive essay
- Use strategies for reading essays

Integrating Skills

Grammar
- Adjective and Adverb Phrases
- Compound Adjectives

Vocabulary
- Using Context Clues
- Connotation and Denotation

Preparing to Read
____ Connect to Your Life
____ Build Background
____ Vocabulary Preview: Using Context Clues   ❑ Unit Three Resource Book: Words to Know SkillBuilder, p. 19
____ Focus Your Reading
Literary Analysis: Essay   ❑ Unit Three Resource Book: Literary Analysis SkillBuilder, p. 18
Active Reading: Strategies for Reading Essays   ❑ Unit Three Resource Book: Active Reading SkillBuilder, p. 17

Teaching the Literature   ❑ PE pp. 369–380
____ Reading the Selection   ❑ Unit Three Resource Book: Summary, p. 16

Thinking Through the Literature
____ Connect to the Literature
____ Think Critically   ❑ Reading and Critical Thinking Transparencies, T15, T20
____ Extend Interpretations
____ Literary Analysis: Essay   ❑ Literary Analysis Transparencies, T8, T9

Choices and Challenges
Writing Options
____ Comparison of Emerson and Thoreau
____ Personal Response
____ Essay on Citizenship

Activities and Explorations
____ Group Discussion
____ Drama in a Jailhouse
____ Political Poster

Inquiry and Research
____ Resisting Injustice

Vocabulary in Action
____ Context Clues

Copyright © McDougal Littell Inc.

Teaching Options (from Teacher's Edition)

Mini Lessons

Preteaching Vocabulary
____ Using Context Clues

Vocabulary Strategy
____ Understanding Connotative and
Denotative Meanings of Words

❑ Vocabulary Transparencies and Copymasters, C38

Grammar
____ Modifiers: Adjective and
Adverb Phrases
____ Compound Adjectives

Viewing and Representing
· Art Appreciation
____ Photographs

Inquiry and Research
____ Generating Relevant Questions

Cross Curricular Links

History
____ U.S.-Mexican War

Social Studies
____ Female Leaders of Social Protest

Informal Assessment
____ Idea Chart

Assessment

____ Selection Quiz
____ Selection Test
____ Test Generator

❑ Unit Three Resource Book: Selection Quiz, p. 20
❑ Formal Assessment: Selection Test, pp. 69–70

Homework Assignments

_____
_____
_____
_____

Other Teaching Materials

_____
_____
_____
_____

Copyright © McDougal Littell Inc.

from Walden

Core Objectives

- Understand and appreciate a classic example of nature writing
- Evaluate the author's observations in an essay

Integrating Skills

Grammar

- Modifiers: *Good* and *Well*
- Modifiers: Nouns as Adjectives
- Double Negatives

Vocabulary

- Using Context Clues
- Homonyms

Preparing to Read

____ Connect to Your Life

____ Build Background

____ Vocabulary Preview: Using Context Clues   ❑ Unit Three Resource Book: Words to Know SkillBuilder, p. 24

____ Focus Your Reading

Literary Analysis: Nature Writing   ❑ Unit Three Resource Book: Literary Analysis SkillBuilder, p. 23

Active Reading: Evaluating Author's   ❑ Unit Three Resource Book: Active Reading SkillBuilder, p. 22
Observations

Teaching the Literature

❑ PE pp. 381–393

____ Reading the Selection   ❑ Unit Three Resource Book: Summary, p. 21

Thinking Through the Literature

____ Connect to the Literature

____ Think Critically   ❑ Reading and Critical Thinking Transparencies, T46

____ Extend Interpretations

____ Literary Analysis: Nature Writing   ❑ Literary Analysis Transparencies, T8, T22

Choices and Challenges

Writing Options

____ Letter from Walden Pond

____ Interpretive Essay

____ Nature Writing

Activities and Explorations

____ Photo Essay

Inquiry and Research

____ Walden Today

Vocabulary in Action

____ Assessment Practice

____ Idioms

Copyright © McDougal Littell Inc.

Teaching Options (from Teacher's Edition)

Mini Lessons

Preteaching Vocabulary
____ Using Context Clues

Vocabulary Strategy
____ Homonyms
    ❑ Vocabulary Transparencies and Copymasters, C35

Grammar
____ Modifiers: *Good* and *Well*
____ Modifiers: Nouns as Adjectives
____ Double Negatives

Viewing and Representing
Art Appreciation
____ Photo by Ernst Haas

Cross Curricular Links

Workplace
____ Setting Goals

Social Studies
____ Nature Conservation

Informal Assessment
____ Make Inferences and Draw Conclusions
____ Journal Entry

Assessment

____ Selection Quiz   ❑ Unit Three Resource Book: Selection Quiz, p. 25
____ Selection Test   ❑ Formal Assessment: Selection Test, pp. 71–72
____ Test Generator

Homework Assignments

_____

_____

_____

_____

_____

Other Teaching Materials

_____

_____

_____

_____

_____

Copyright © McDougal Littell Inc.

Selected Poems by Walt Whitman

Core Objectives
- Understand and appreciate three classic poems
- Identify and understand free verse and Whitman's poetic devices for creating rhythm
- Apply strategies for reading free verse

Integrating Skills

Grammar
- Prepositional Phrases
- Placement of Prepositional Phrases

Vocabulary
- Understanding Analogies

Preparing to Read

____ Connect to Your Life

____ Build Background

____ Focus Your Reading

Literary Analysis: Free Verse   ❑ Unit Three Resource Book: Literary Analysis SkillBuilder, p. 27

Active Reading: Strategies for Reading   ❑ Unit Three Resource Book: Active Reading SkillBuilder, p. 26
     Free Verse

Teaching the Literature

____ Reading the Selection   ❑ PE pp. 396–405

Thinking Through the Literature

____ Connect to the Literature

____ Think Critically   ❑ Reading and Critical Thinking Transparencies, T15

____ Extend Interpretations

____ Literary Analysis: Free Verse   ❑ Literary Analysis Transparencies, T12

Choices and Challenges

Writing Options

____ Literary Review

____ Free Verse Poem

Activities and Explorations

____ Collage of Images

____ Interpretive Dance

Author Activity

____ Neruda's Whitman

Copyright © McDougal Littell Inc.

Teaching Options (from Teacher's Edition)

Mini Lessons

Vocabulary Strategy

____ Understanding Analogies ❑ Vocabulary Transparencies and Copymasters, C48

Grammar

____ Prepositional Phrases ❑ Grammar Transparencies and Copymasters, T11, C83, C84
____ Placement of Prepositional Phrases

Speaking and Listening

____ Choral Reading

Viewing and Representing

Art Appreciation
____ *Cliff Dwellers* by George Bellows

Cross Curricular Link

History

____ Urban and Rural Life—1800s and Today

Assessment

____ Selection Test ❑ Formal Assessment: Selection Test, pp. 73–74
____ Test Generator

Homework Assignments

_____
_____
_____
_____

Other Teaching Materials

_____
_____
_____

Copyright © McDougal Littell Inc.

Danse Russe / anyone lived in a pretty how town   Pages 410–415

Core Objectives
■ Understand and appreciate experimental poetry
■ Make inferences to understand poetry

Preparing to Read
____ Comparing Literature
____ Build Background
____ Focus Your Reading
     Literary Analysis: Experimental Poetry   ❑ Unit Three Resource Book: Literary Analysis SkillBuilder, p. 29
     Active Reading: Making Inferences   ❑ Unit Three Resource Book: Active Reading SkillBuilder, p. 28

Teaching the Literature
____ Reading the Selection   ❑ PE pp. 410–415

Thinking Through the Literature
____ Connect to the Literature
____ Think Critically   ❑ Reading and Critical Thinking Transparencies, T7
____ Extend Interpretations
____ Literary Analysis: Experimental Poetry   ❑ Literary Analysis Transparencies, T12

Choices and Challenges

Writing Options
____ Diary Confession
____ Headstone Inscription
____ Points of Comparison

Activities and Explorations
____ Animation, Anyone?

Author Activity
____ Williams on Video
____ Cummings's Voice

Copyright © McDougal Littell Inc.

Danse Russe / anyone lived in a pretty how town

Teaching Options (from Teacher's Edition)

Mini Lessons

Speaking and Listening
____ Interpreting Poems

Viewing and Representing
____ Art Appreciation
____ *Icarus* by Henri Matisse

Informal Assessment
____ Identifying and Comparing Themes

Assessment

____ Selection Test

____ Test Generator

❑ Formal Assessment: Selection Test, pp. 75–76

Homework Assignments

_____

_____

_____

_____

_____

Other Teaching Materials

_____

_____

_____

_____

_____

Copyright © McDougal Littell Inc.

Ending Poem / Tia Chucha

Core Objectives
- Understand and appreciate poetry that explores cultural and individual identity
- Identify and understand the speaker of a poem
- Understand structure and form in poetry

Integrating Skills
Vocabulary
- Using Reference Materials

Preparing to Read
____ Comparing Literature
____ Build Background
____ Focus Your Reading
     Literary Analysis: Speaker   ❏ Unit Three Resource Book: Literary Analysis SkillBuilder, p. 31
     Active Reading: Structure and Form in Poetry   ❏ Unit Three Resource Book: Active Reading SkillBuilder, p. 30

Teaching the Literature
____ Reading the Selection   ❏ PE pp. 416–423

Thinking Through the Literature
____ Connect to the Literature
____ Think Critically   ❏ Reading and Critical Thinking Transparencies, T15
____ Extend Interpretations
____ Literary Analysis: Speaker   ❏ Literary Analysis Transparencies, T11, T20

Choices and Challenges
Writing Options
____ Points of Comparison
____ Autobiographical Sketch or Poem
____ Contrast Essay

Activities and Explorations
____ Paired Reading
____ Monologue
____ Self-Representation

____ ### Art Connection

Inquiry and Research
____ Puerto Rican History

Copyright © McDougal Littell Inc.

Teaching Options (from Teacher's Edition)

Mini Lessons

Vocabulary Strategy
____ Using Reference Materials

❏ Vocabulary Transparencies and Copymasters: C40

Speaking and Listening
____ Pronouncing Spanish Words

Viewing and Representing
Art Appreciation
____ *In My Grandmother's Garden*
by Rosario Morales

Cross Curricular Link

History
____ The Chicano Movement

Informal Assessment
____ Figurative Language

Assessment
____ Selection Test
____ Test Generator

❏ Formal Assessment: Selection Test: pp. 77–78

Homework Assignments
_____
_____
_____
_____

Other Teaching Materials
_____
_____
_____
_____
_____

Copyright © McDougal Littell Inc.

Core Objectives
- Understand and appreciate an autobiographical story
- Identify examples of humor in the story
- Consider the purpose for reading the story

Integrating Skills

Grammar
- Appositives and Appositive Phrases
- Commas and Parenthetical Expressions

Vocabulary
- Using Context to Determine Meaning of Idioms

Preparing to Read
____ Comparing Literature
____ Build Background
____ Focus Your Reading
      Literary Analysis: Humor   ❑ Unit Three Resource Book: Literary Analysis SkillBuilder, p. 34
      Active Reading: Purpose For Reading   ❑ Unit Three Resource Book: Active Reading SkillBuilder, p. 33

Teaching the Literature
                                ❑ PE pp. 424–435
____ Reading the Selection   ❑ Unit Three Resource Book: Summary, p. 32

Thinking Through the Literature
____ Connect to the Literature
____ Think Critically   ❑ Reading and Critical Thinking Transparencies, T23
____ Extend Interpretations
____ Literary Analysis: Humor

Choices and Challenges

Writing Options
____ Points of Comparison
____ Story Sequel
____ Literary Review

Activities and Explorations
____ Drawn-Out Story
____ Comic Recitation

____ Art Connection

Author Activity
____ Good Humor

Copyright © McDougal Littell Inc.

Gary Keillor

Teaching Options (from Teacher's Edition)

Mini Lessons

Vocabulary Strategy
____ Using Context to Determine Meaning of Idioms

❑ Vocabulary Transparencies and Copymasters, C41

Grammar
____ Appositives and Appositive Phrases

❑ Grammar Transparencies and Copymasters, C85

____ Commas with Parenthetical Expressions

❑ Grammar Transparencies and Copymasters, C148

Speaking and Listening
____ Radio Performance

Viewing and Representing
Art Appreciation
____ *Play Within a Play* by David Hockney

Cross Curricular Link

Social Studies
____ Oral Storytelling

Informal Assessment
____ Journal Entries

Assessment
____ Selection Quiz

❑ Unit Three Resource Book: Selection Quiz, p. 35

____ Selection Test

❑ Formal Assessment: Selection Test, pp. 79-80

____ Part Test

❑ Formal Assessment: Unit Three, Part 1 Test, pp. 81–82

____ Test Generator

Homework Assignments

_____
_____
_____
_____
_____

Other Teaching Materials

_____
_____
_____
_____
_____

Copyright © McDougal Littell Inc.

Reflective Essay

Writing Prompt

Write an essay in which you reflect on an
experience that taught you an important lesson.

Preparing

____ Introduction
____ Basics in a Box
____ Using the Graphic

❑ Writing Transparencies and Copymasters, T11, T20, C28

____ Analyzing a Student Model
    "Eternally Slow"

❑ Unit Three Resource Book: Student Models, pp. 42–47

Writing

____ **Prewriting**
    Choosing a Subject
    Planning the Reflective Essay

❑ Unit Three Resource Book: Prewriting, p. 37

____ **Drafting**
    Organizing the Draft

❑ Unit Three Resource Book: Drafting and Elaboration, p. 38

____ **Peer Review**
    Ask Your Peer Reader

❑ Unit Three Resource Book: Peer Response Guide, pp. 39–40

____ **Revising**
    Avoiding Clichés

❑ Unit Three Resource Book: Revising, Editing, and Proofreading, p. 41
❑ Unit Three Resource Book: Rubric for Evaluation, p. 48

____ **Editing and Proofreading**
    Possessives and Plurals

____ **Reflecting**

Copyright © McDougal Littell Inc.

Homework Assignments	**Other Teaching Materials**
_____	_____
_____	_____
_____	_____
_____	_____

The Masque of the Red Death

Core Objectives
- Understand and appreciate a classic short story
- Recognize and interpret allegory
- Clarify meaning in a short story

Integrating Skills

Grammar
- Participles and Participial Phrases
- Past and Present Participles

Vocabulary
- Context Clues
- Latin Root Words

Preparing to Read
____ Connect to Your Life
____ Build Background
____ Vocabulary Preview: Using Context Clues   ❑ Unit Three Resource Book: Words to Know SkillBuilder, p. 54
____ Focus Your Reading
       Literary Analysis: Allegory   ❑ Unit Three Resource Book: Literary Analysis SkillBuilder, p. 53
       Active Reading: Clarifying Meaning   ❑ Unit Three Resource Book: Active Reading SkillBuilder, p. 52

Teaching the Literature
____ Reading the Selection   ❑ PE pp. 454–463

Thinking Through the Literature
____ Connect to the Literature
____ Think Critically   ❑ Reading and Critical Thinking Transparencies, T10
____ Extend Interpretations
____ Literary Analysis: Allegory

Choices and Challenges

Writing Options
____ Newspaper Editorial
____ Poetic Retelling
____ Archaeological Report

Activities and Explorations
____ A Fantastic Set
____ Radio Drama

Inquiry and Research
____ Medical Detective

Vocabulary in Action
____ Word Knowledge

Copyright © McDougal Littell Inc.

The Masque of the Red Death

Teaching Options (from Teacher's Edition)

Mini Lessons

Preteaching Vocabulary
____ Using Context Clues

Vocabulary Strategy
____ Applying Meanings of Latin Root Words ☐ Vocabulary Transparencies and Copymasters, C42

Grammar
____ Participles and Participial Phrases ☐ Grammar Transparencies and Copymasters, C86
____ Using Past and Present Participles ☐ Grammar Transparencies and Copymasters, C87

Speaking and Listening
____ Nonverbal Communication

Viewing and Representing
Art Appreciation
____ *Il ridotto [The Foyer]* by Pietro Longhi

Informal Assessment
____ Storyboard

Assessment
____ Selection Quiz ☐ Unit Three Resource Book: Selection Quiz, p. 55
____ Selection Test ☐ Formal Assessment: Selection Test, pp. 83–84
____ Test Generator

Homework Assignments	Other Teaching Materials

Copyright © McDougal Littell Inc.

Core Objectives

- Understand and appreciate a classic narrative poem
- Identify and analyze sound devices in a poem
- Draw conclusions about the speaker in a poem

Integrating Skills

Grammar   **Vocabulary**
- Comparative Forms   - Using Context Clues
  of Adjectives and
  Adverbs

Preparing to Read

___ Connect to Your Life
___ Build Background
___ Vocabulary Preview: Using Context Clues   ❏ Unit Three Resource Book: Words to Know SkillBuilder, p. 59
___ Focus Your Reading
    Literary Analysis: Sound Devices   ❏ Unit Three Resource Book: Literary Analysis SkillBuilder, p. 58
    Active Reading: Drawing Conclusions   ❏ Unit Three Resource Book: Active Reading SkillBuilder, p. 57

Teaching the Literature   ❏ PE pp. 466–472
___ Reading the Selection   ❏ Unit Three Resource Book: Summary, p. 56

Thinking Through the Literature

___ Connect to the Literature
___ Think Critically   ❏ Reading and Critical Thinking Transparencies, T4
___ Extend Interpretations
___ Literary Analysis: Sound Devices   ❏ Literary Analysis Transparencies, T12

Choices and Challenges

Writing Options
___ Prose Description
___ Speaker's Diary Entry
___ Poetic Parody

Activities and Explorations
___ Dramatic Reading
___ Image of the Study

Inquiry and Research
___ Psychological View

Vocabulary in Action
___ Meaning Clues

Copyright © McDougal Littell Inc.

The Raven

Teaching Options (from Teacher's Edition)

Mini Lessons

Preteaching Vocabulary
____ Using Context Clues

Grammar
____ Comparative Forms of Adjectives and Adverbs

❑ Grammar Transparencies and Copymasters, C128

Speaking and Listening
____ Dramatic Reading

Informal Assessment
____ Evaluating the Speaker

Assessment
____ Selection Quiz
____ Selection Test
____ Test Generator

❑ Unit Three Resource Book: Selection Quiz, p. 60
❑ Formal Assessment: Selection Test, pp. 85–86

Homework Assignments

_____

_____

_____

_____

_____

Other Teaching Materials

_____

_____

_____

_____

_____

Copyright © McDougal Littell Inc.

The Fall of the House of Usher

Core Objectives
- Understand and appreciate a classic Gothic short story
- Identify and understand mood in a short story
- Understand complex sentences

Integrating Skills

Grammar
- Irregular Adjectives and Adverbs
- Apostrophes: Possessive Compounds
- Dashes

Vocabulary
- Context Clues
- Understanding Prefixes
- Understanding Figurative Language

Preparing to Read
____ Connect to Your Life
____ Build Background
____ Vocabulary Preview: Using Context Clues   ❑ Unit Three Resource Book: Words to Know SkillBuilder, p. 64
____ Focus Your Reading
      Literary Analysis: Mood   ❑ Unit Three Resource Book: Literary Analysis SkillBuilder, p. 63
      Active Reading: Understanding Complex   ❑ Unit Three Resource Book: Active Reading SkillBuilder, p. 62
         Sentences

Teaching the Literature
❑ PE pp. 473–499
____ Reading the Selection   ❑ Unit Three Resource Book: Summary, p. 61

Thinking Through the Literature
____ Connect to the Literature
____ Think Critically   ❑ Reading and Critical Thinking Transparencies, T12, T15, T49
____ Extend Interpretations
____ Literary Analysis: Mood   ❑ Literary Analysis Transparencies, T18

Choices and Challenges

Writing Options
____ Roderick Usher's Letter
____ Comparing Ushers
____ Madeline's Retelling

Activities and Explorations
____ Eerie Pantomime
____ Usher Poster
____ Charting Usher Events

Inquiry and Research
____ Science

Vocabulary in Action
____ Context Clues/Meaning Clues

Copyright © McDougal Littell Inc.

The Fall of the House of Usher

Teaching Options (from Teacher's Edition)

Mini Lessons

Preteaching Vocabulary

____ Using Context Clues

Vocabulary Strategy

____ Understanding Prefixes ❑ Vocabulary Transparencies and Copymasters, C44

____ Understanding Figurative Language

Grammar

____ Comparisons of Irregular Adjectives and ❑ Grammar Transparencies and Copymasters, T52, C129
Adverbs

____ Apostrophes: Possessive Compounds ❑ Grammar Transparencies and Copymasters, C160

____ Dashes ❑ Grammar Transparencies and Copymasters, C161

Speaking and Listening

____ Oral Reading

____ Dramatic Reading

Viewing and Representing

Art Appreciation

____ *Self Portrait* by Bertalan Szekely

____ *Head of Ophelia* by Edwin Austin Abbey

Cross Curricular Links

Humanities

____ Gothic Architecture

Psychology

____ Twins

Informal Assessment

____ Describing Plot, Setting, Character, and Mood

____ Journal Entry

Assessment

____ Selection Quiz ❑ Unit Three Resource Book: Selection Quiz, p. 65

____ Selection Test ❑ Formal Assessment: Selection Test, pp. 87–88

____ Test Generator

Homework Assignments	Other Teaching Materials

Copyright © McDougal Littell Inc.

Dr. Heidegger's Experiment

Core Objectives
- Understand and appreciate a classic short story that explores a Gothic theme
- Identify and understand foreshadowing
- Interpret the story as an allegory

Integrating Skills

Grammar
- Comparatives
- Avoiding Illogical Comparisons

Vocabulary
- Using Context Clues
- Applying Meaning of Suffixes

Preparing to Read
____ Connect to Your Life
____ Build Background
____ Vocabulary Preview: Using Context Clues ❑ Unit Three Resource Book: Words to Know SkillBuilder, p. 69
____ Focus Your Reading
     Literary Analysis: Foreshadowing ❑ Unit Three Resource Book: Literary Analysis SkillBuilder, p. 68
     Active Reading: Interpreting Allegory ❑ Unit Three Resource Book: Active Reading SkillBuilder, p. 67

Teaching the Literature
❑ PE pp. 500–515
____ Reading the Selection ❑ Unit Three Resource Book: Summary, p. 66

Thinking Through the Literature
____ Connect to the Literature
____ Think Critically ❑ Reading and Critical Thinking Transparencies, T2, T15
____ Extend Interpretations
____ Literary Analysis: Foreshadowing

Choices and Challenges

Writing Options
____ Warning Label
____ Science News
____ Story Ending

Activities and Explorations
____ Product Chart

Vocabulary in Action
____ Assessment Practice

Copyright © McDougal Littell Inc.

Dr. Heidegger's Experiment

Teaching Options (from Teacher's Edition)

Mini Lessons

Preteaching Vocabulary
____ Using Context Clues

Vocabulary Strategy
____ Applying Meanings of Suffixes

❑ Vocabulary Transparencies and Copymasters, C46

Grammar
____ Comparatives
____ Avoiding Illogical Comparisons

Speaking and Listening
____ Interpreting Character

Viewing and Representing
Art Appreciation
____ *Déjeuner [Luncheon]* by Gustave Caillebotte
____ *La Danse à la Campagne [The country dance]* by Pierre Auguste Renoir

Cross Curricular Links

History
____ Ponce de Leon and the Fountain of Youth

Multicultural
____ Attitudes Toward Aging

Informal Assessment
____ Changing Point of View
____ Choosing the Best Summary

Assessment

____ Selection Quiz
____ Selection Test
____ Test Generator

❑ Unit Three Resource Book: Selection Quiz, p. 70
❑ Formal Assessment: Selection Test, pp. 89–90

Homework Assignments

_____
_____
_____
_____

Other Teaching Materials

_____
_____
_____
_____

Copyright © McDougal Littell Inc.

A Rose for Emily

Core Objectives
- Understand and appreciate a short story
- Identify and understand characterization
- Understand the sequence of events in the story

Integrating Skills

Grammar
- Superlatives
- Modifiers: Illogical Comparisons

Vocabulary
- Using Context Clues
- Connotation

Preparing to Read
____ Comparing Literature
____ Build Background
____ Vocabulary Preview: Using Context Clues   ❑ Unit Three Resource Book: Words to Know SkillBuilder, p. 74
____ Focus Your Reading
     Literary Analysis: Characterization   ❑ Unit Three Resource Book: Literary Analysis SkillBuilder, p. 73
     Active Reading: Sequencing Events   ❑ Unit Three Resource Book: Active Reading SkillBuilder, p. 72

Teaching the Literature
     ❑ PE pp. 516–527
____ Reading the Selection   ❑ Unit Three Resource Book: Summary, p. 71

Thinking Through the Literature
____ Connect to the Literature
____ Think Critically   ❑ Reading and Critical Thinking Transparencies, T13, T15
____ Extend Interpretations
____ Literary Analysis: Foreshadowing   ❑ Literary Analysis Transparencies, T6

Choices and Challenges

Writing Options
____ Obituary for Miss Emily
____ Secret Diary
____ Points of Comparison

Activities and Explorations
____ Short Story Video
____ Theatrical Performance

Inquiry and Research
____ The New South

Vocabulary in Action
____ Context Clues

Copyright © McDougal Littell Inc.

A Rose for Emily

Teaching Options (from Teacher's Edition)

Mini Lessons

Preteaching Vocabulary
____ Using Context Clues

Vocabulary Strategy
____ Connotation

❏ Vocabulary Transparencies and Copymasters, C47

Grammar
____ Superlatives
____ Modifiers: Illogical Comparisons

Speaking and Listening
____ Dramatic Performance

Viewing and Representing
Art Appreciation
____ *German Teapot* by Charles Warren Mundy
____ *Woman in Distress* by James Ensor

Cross Curricular Link

Workplace
____ Writing Instructions/Problem Solving

Informal Assessment
____ News Report

Assessment
____ Selection Quiz
____ Selection Test
____ Test Generator

❏ Unit Three Resource Book: Selection Quiz, p. 75
❏ Formal Assessment: Selection Test, pp. 91–92

Homework Assignments

_____

_____

_____

_____

_____

Other Teaching Materials

_____

_____

_____

_____

Copyright © McDougal Littell Inc.

The Life You Save May Be Your Own

Core Objectives
- Understand and appreciate a Southern Gothic short story
- Identify and examine irony
- Draw conclusions about characters

Integrating Skills

Grammar
- Modifiers:
  Double Negatives

Vocabulary
- Using Context Clues
- Analogies

Preparing to Read
____ Comparing Literature
____ Build Background
____ Vocabulary Preview: Using Context Clues   ❑ Unit Three Resource Book: Words to Know SkillBuilder, p. 79
____ Focus Your Reading
Literary Analysis: Irony   ❑ Unit Three Resource Book: Literary Analysis SkillBuilder, p. 78
Active Reading: Drawing Conclusions   ❑ Unit Three Resource Book: Active Reading SkillBuilder, p. 77
　　About Characters

Teaching the Literature
____ Reading the Selection   ❑ PE pp. 528–541
____ Reading the Selection   ❑ Unit Three Resource Book: Summary, p. 76

Thinking Through the Literature
____ Connect to the Literature
____ Think Critically   ❑ Reading and Critical Thinking Transparencies, T4
____ Extend Interpretations
____ Literary Analysis: Irony   ❑ Literary Analysis Transparencies, T21

Choices and Challenges

Writing Options
____ Letter of Opinion
____ Sequel: The Saga Continues
____ Points of Comparison

Activities and Explorations
____ Wanted Poster
____ Points of Comparison

Inquiry and Research
____ Con Artists
____ Antisocial Personalities

Vocabulary in Action
____ Assessment Practice

Author Activity
____ The Writer's Eye

Copyright © McDougal Littell Inc.

The Life You Save May Be Your Own

Teaching Options (from Teacher's Edition)

Mini Lessons

Preteaching Vocabulary

____ Using Context Clues

Vocabulary Strategy

____ Analogies   ❑ Vocabulary Transparencies and Copymasters, C48

Grammar

____ Modifiers: Double Negatives ❑ Grammar Transparencies and Copymasters, T53, C137

Speaking and Listening

____ Dramatic Presentation

Viewing and Representing

Art Appreciation

____ *Mrs. Gamely* by George Luks

____ *The Interloper* by Billy Morrow Jackson

____ *Road to Rhome* by Alexander Hogue

Cross Curricular Link

History

____ Henry Ford

Informal Assessment

____ Making Inferences

____ Storyboard

Assessment

____ Selection Quiz   ❑ Unit Three Resource Book: Selection Quiz, p. 80

____ Selection Test   ❑ Formal Assessment: Selection Test, pp. 93–94

____ Part Test   ❑ Formal Assessment: Unit Three, Part 2 Test, pp. 95–96

____ Test Generator

Homework Assignments

_____

_____

_____

_____

_____

Other Teaching Materials

_____

_____

_____

_____

_____

Copyright © McDougal Littell Inc.

Writing Prompt

Write a short story. You might choose
to use a surprise ending or twist.

_____

Preparing

____ Introduction

____ Basics in a Box

____ Using the Graphic

❑ Writing Transparencies and Copymasters, T11, T20, C29

____ Analyzing a Student Model
"Reunited"

❑ Unit Three Resource Book: Student Models, pp. 87–92

Writing

____ **Prewriting**
Choosing a Story Idea
Planning the Short Story

❑ Unit Three Resource Book: Prewriting, p. 82

____ **Drafting**
Organizing the Draft

❑ Unit Three Resource Book: Drafting and Elaboration, p. 83

____ **Peer Review**
Ask Your Peer Reader

❑ Unit Three Resource Book: Peer Response Guide, pp. 84–85

____ **Revising**
Using Dialogue

❑ Unit Three Resource Book: Revising, Editing, and Proofreading, p. 86
❑ Unit Three Resource Book: Rubric for Evaluation, p. 93

____ **Editing and Proofreading**
Punctuating Dialogue

____ **Reflecting**

_____

Homework Assignments

_____

_____

_____

_____

_____

Other Teaching Materials

_____

_____

_____

_____

_____

Copyright © McDougal Littell Inc.

Narrative of the Life of Frederick Douglass
Pages 562–573

Core Objectives
- Understand and appreciate a slave narrative
- Examine autobiography and style
- Analyze author's purpose

Integrating Skills

Grammar
- Identifying Clauses: Independent and Subordinate

Vocabulary
- Context Clues
- Connotation/Denotation

Preparing to Read
___ Connect to Your Life
___ Build Background
___ Vocabulary Preview: Using Context Clues   ❑ Unit Four Resource Book: Words to Know SkillBuilder, p. 7
___ Focus Your Reading
      Literary Analysis: Autobiography and Style   ❑ Unit Four Resource Book: Literary Analysis SkillBuilder, p. 6
      Active Reading: Author's Purpose   ❑ Unit Four Resource Book: Active Reading SkillBuilder, p. 5

Teaching the Literature
                                                     ❑ PE pp. 562–573
___ Reading the Selection   ❑ Unit Four Resource Book: Summary, p. 4

Thinking Through the Literature
___ Connect to the Literature
___ Think Critically   ❑ Reading and Critical Thinking Transparencies, T19
___ Extend Interpretations
___ Literary Analysis: Autobiography and Style   ❑ Literary Analysis Transparencies, T23

Choices and Challenges

Writing Options
___ Closing Statement
___ Antislavery Editorial
___ Comparison of Slave Narratives
___ Autobiographical Sketch

Activities and Explorations
___ Living to Tell
___ Story in Pictures
___ Discussion of Covey

Inquiry and Research
___ Another View
___ Slave Laws

Copyright © McDougal Littell Inc.

Narrative of the Life of Frederick Douglass

Choices and Challenges (continued)
Vocabulary in Action
____ Meaning Clues

Author Activity
____ Poetic Tribute
____ Art Connection

Teaching Options (from Teacher's Edition)
Mini Lessons

Preteaching Vocabulary
____ Using Context Clues

Vocabulary Strategy
____ Connotation/Denotation

❏ Vocabulary Transparencies and Copymasters, C49

Grammar
____ Identifying Clauses: Independent and Subordinate

❏ Grammar Transparencies and Copymasters, C88

Speaking and Listening
____ Persuasive Speech

Viewing and Representing
Art Appreciation
____ *Head of a Negro* by John Singleton Copley

Cross Curricular Link
____ History

Informal Assessment
____ Summarizing

Assessment
____ Selection Quiz
____ Selection Test
____ Test Generator

❏ Unit Four Resource Book: Selection Quiz, p. 8
❏ Formal Assessment: Selection Test, p. 105–106

Homework Assignments

Other Teaching Materials

Copyright © McDougal Littell Inc.

Stanzas on Freedom / Free Labor

Core Objectives
- Understand and appreciate protest poems that explore the meaning of freedom and slavery
- Identify and appreciate symbols in a poem
- Apply strategies for reading protest poetry

Integrating Skills

Grammar
- Clauses vs. Phrases

Vocabulary
- Understanding Figurative Language Through Context

Preparing to Read
____ Connect to Your Life
____ Build Background
____ Focus Your Reading
    Literary Analysis: Symbol
    Active Reading: Strategies for Reading
      Protest Poetry

❑ Unit Four Resource Book: Literary Analysis SkillBuilder, p. 10
❑ Unit Four Resource Book: Active Reading SkillBuilder, p. 9

Teaching the Literature
____ Reading the Selection

❑ PE pp. 574–579

Thinking Through the Literature
____ Connect to the Literature
____ Think Critically
____ Extend Interpretations
____ Literary Analysis: Symbol

Choices and Challenges

Writing Options
____ New Stanza
____ Protest Poem

Activities and Explorations
____ Political Poster

Copyright © McDougal Littell Inc.

Stanzas on Freedom / Free Labor

Teaching Options (from Teacher's Edition)

Mini Lessons

Vocabulary Strategy

____ Understanding Figurative Language   ❑ Vocabulary Transparencies and Copymasters, C50
Through Context

Grammar

____ Clauses vs. Phrases   ❑ Grammar Transparencies and Copymasters, C90

Speaking and Listening

____ Dramatic Reading

Informal Assessment

____ Contrasting Across Texts

Assessment

____ Selection Test   ❑ Formal Assessment: Selection Test, pp. 107–108

____ Test Generator

Homework Assignments	Other Teaching Materials

Copyright © McDougal Littell Inc.

An Occurrence at Owl Creek Bridge

Core Objectives
- Appreciate a short story about the Civil War
- Identify and examine point of view
- Analyze structure in a short story

Integrating Skills

Grammar
- Essential vs. Nonessential Clauses
- Punctuation for Clauses

Vocabulary
- Context Clues
- Applying Meaning of Prefixes

Preparing to Read
___ Connect to Your Life
___ Build Background
___ Vocabulary Preview: Using Context Clues   ❑ Unit Four Resource Book: Words to Know SkillBuilder, p. 14
___ Focus Your Reading
     Literary Analysis: Point of View   ❑ Unit Four Resource Book: Literary Analysis SkillBuilder, p. 13
     Active Reading: Analyzing Structure   ❑ Unit Four Resource Book: Active Reading SkillBuilder, p. 12

Teaching the Literature
     ❑ PE pp. 580–592
___ Reading the Selection   ❑ Unit Four Resource Book: Summary, p. 11

Thinking Through the Literature
___ Connect to the Literature
___ Think Critically   ❑ Reading and Critical Thinking Transparencies, T6, T17
___ Extend Interpretations
___ Literary Analysis: Point of View   ❑ Literary Analysis Transparencies, T20

Choices and Challenges
Writing Options
___ Evaluation of Bierce
___ Comparison Essay

Vocabulary in Action
___ Synonyms

Copyright © McDougal Littell Inc.

Teaching Options (from Teacher's Edition)

Mini Lessons

Preteaching Vocabulary
____ Using Context Clues

Vocabulary Strategy
____ Applying Meanings of Prefixes   ❏ Vocabulary Transparencies and Copymasters, C51

Grammar
____ Essential vs. Nonessential Clauses   ❏ Grammar Transparencies and Copymasters, T44, C91
____ Punctuation for Clauses   ❏ Grammar Transparencies and Copymasters, T55, C149

Speaking and Listening
____ Realistic Dialogue

Viewing and Representing
Art Appreciation
____ *Union Soldiers* by anonymous
____ Story Illustrations

Cross Curricular Link

History
____ The 54th Regiment

Informal Assessment
____ Self-Assessment

Assessment
____ Selection Quiz   ❏ Unit Four Resource Book: Selection Quiz, p. 15
____ Selection Test   ❏ Formal Assessment: Selection Test, pp. 109–110
____ Test Generator

Homework Assignments

_____

_____

_____

_____

Other Teaching Materials

_____

_____

_____

_____

Copyright © McDougal Littell Inc.

A Mystery of Heroism

Core Objectives

- Understand and appreciate a short story
- Identify characteristics of naturalism in the story
- Visualize the setting, characters, and events in the story

Integrating Skills

Grammar
- Introduction to Adjective Clauses
- Use of Commas in Names and Titles

Vocabulary
- Using Context Clues
- Root Words

Preparing to Read

____ Connect to Your Life
____ Build Background
____ Vocabulary Preview: Using Context Clues   ❑ Unit Four Resource Book: Words to Know SkillBuilder, p. 19
____ Focus Your Reading
     Literary Analysis: Naturalism   ❑ Unit Four Resource Book: Literary Analysis SkillBuilder, p. 18
     Active Reading: Visualizing   ❑ Unit Four Resource Book: Active Reading SkillBuilder, p. 17

Teaching the Literature

❑ PE pp. 593–604
____ Reading the Selection   ❑ Unit Four Resource Book: Summary, p. 16

Thinking Through the Literature

____ Connect to the Literature
____ Think Critically   ❑ Reading and Critical Thinking Transparencies, T8
____ Extend Interpretations
____ Literary Analysis: Naturalism

Choices and Challenges

Writing Options
____ Letter Home
____ Literary Analysis
____ Different Ending

Activities and Explorations
____ Combat Sketch
____ War Songs
____ Interview with Collins

Inquiry and Research
____ Photo Gallery

Vocabulary in Action
____ Meaning Clues

Author Activity
____ War Stories

Copyright © McDougal Littell Inc.

Teaching Options (from Teacher's Edition)

Mini Lessons

Preteaching Vocabulary
___ Using Context Clues

Vocabulary Strategy
___ Root Words
❑ Vocabulary Transparencies and Copymasters, C52

Grammar
___ Introduction to Adjective Clauses
❑ Grammar Transparencies and Copymasters, C92
___ Use of Commas in Names and Titles
❑ Grammar Transparencies and Copymasters, C150

Speaking and Listening
___ Persuasive Speaking

Viewing and Representing
Art Appreciation
___ *The Battle of Chancellorsville*
by unknown artist

Cross Curricular Link

History
___ Parallel Naturalist Movements in Other Cultures

Informal Assessment
___ Identifying Supporting Ideas

Assessment
___ Selection Quiz
❑ Unit Four Resource Book: Selection Quiz, p. 20
___ Selection Test
❑ Formal Assessment: Selection Test, pp. 111–112
___ Test Generator

Homework Assignments

_____
_____
_____
_____
_____

Other Teaching Materials

_____
_____
_____
_____
_____

Copyright © McDougal Littell Inc.

The Gettysburg Address

Core Objectives
- Understand and appreciate a classic speech
- Identify and examine style in a speech
- Appreciate historical context in a speech

Integrating Skills

Grammar
- Adjective and Relative Clauses

Vocabulary
- Context Clues

Preparing to Read

____ Connect to Your Life

____ Build Background

____ Vocabulary Preview: Using Context Clues   ❏ Unit Four Resource Book: Words to Know SkillBuilder, p. 24

____ Focus Your Reading

Literary Analysis: Style   ❏ Unit Four Resource Book: Literary Analysis SkillBuilder, p. 23

Active Reading: Interpreting Historical Context   ❏ Unit Four Resource Book: Active Reading SkillBuilder, p. 22

Teaching the Literature

❏ PE pp. 605–608

____ Reading the Selection   ❏ Unit Four Resource Book: Summary, p. 21

Thinking Through the Literature

____ Connect to the Literature

____ Think Critically   ❏ Reading and Critical Thinking Transparency, T41

____ Extend Interpretations

____ Literary Analysis: Style   ❏ Literary Analysis Transparencies, T23

Choices and Challenges

Writing Options

____ Modern Paraphrase

____ Letter to Lincoln

Inquiry and Research

____ Battle Report

Vocabulary in Action

____ Context Clues

Copyright © McDougal Littell Inc.

The Gettysburg Address

Teaching Options (from Teacher's Edition)

Mini Lesson

Preteaching Vocabulary
____ Using Context Clues

Grammar
____ Adjective and Relative Clauses ❑ Grammar Transparencies and Copymasters, T44, C95

Assessment

____ Selection Quiz ❑ Unit Four Resource Book: Selection Quiz, p. 25
____ Selection Test ❑ Formal Assessment: Selection Test, pp. 113–114
____ Test Generator

Homework Assignments	Other Teaching Materials

Copyright © McDougal Littell Inc.

Coming of Age in Mississippi

Core Objectives
- Appreciate a selection from an autobiography
- Understand an eyewitness report
- Use chronological order to understand an eyewitness report

Integrating Skills

Grammar
- Adverb Clauses
- Punctuation of Adverb Clauses

Vocabulary
- Sensory Details

Preparing to Read
____ Connect to Your Life
____ Build Background
____ Focus Your Reading
    Literary Analysis: Eyewitness Report   ❑ Unit Four Resource Book: Literary Analysis SkillBuilder, p. 28
    Active Reading: Chronological Order   ❑ Unit Four Resource Book: Active Reading SkillBuilder, p. 27

Teaching the Literature
                                  ❑ PE pp. 609–617
____ Reading the Selection   ❑ Unit Four Resource Book: Summary, p. 26

Thinking Through the Literature
____ Connect to the Literature
____ Think Critically   ❑ Reading and Critical Thinking Transparencies, T17, T49
____ Extend Interpretations
____ Literary Analysis: Eyewitness Report   ❑ Literary Analysis Transparencies, T16

Choices and Challenges

Writing Options
____ Mother's Letter, Anne's Reply
____ Points of Comparison
____ Eyewitness Account

Activities and Explorations
____ On the Scene

Art Connection
____ Under Siege

____ **Author Activity**

Copyright © McDougal Littell Inc.

Coming of Age in Mississippi

Teaching Options (from Teacher's Edition)

Mini Lessons

Vocabulary Strategy

____ Sensory Details ❑ Vocabulary Transparencies and Copymasters, C53

Grammar

____ Adverb Clauses ❑ Grammar Transparencies and Copymasters, C96

____ Punctuation of Adverb Clauses ❑ Grammar Transparencies and Copymasters, C151

Viewing and Representing

Art Appreciation

____ Photograph

Cross Curricular Link

____ History

Informal Assessment

____ Literary Response

Assessment

____ Selection Quiz ❑ Unit Four Resource Book: Selection Quiz, p. 29

____ Selection Test ❑ Formal Assessment: Selection Test, pp. 115–116

____ Test Generator

Homework Assignments

Other Teaching Materials

Copyright © McDougal Littell Inc.

Name _____ Date _____

Ballad of Birmingham

Core Objectives
- Understand and appreciate a ballad commemorating a tragic event
- Identify and appreciate the characteristics of ballads
- Apply strategies for reading narrative poetry

Integrating Skills
Grammar
- Introduction to Noun Clauses

Preparing to Read
____ Connect to Your Life
____ Build Background
____ Focus Your Reading
    Literary Analysis: Ballads   ❑ Unit Four Resource Book: Literary Analysis SkillBuilder, p. 31
    Active Reading: Reading Narrative Poetry   ❑ Unit Four Resource Book: Active Reading SkillBuilder, p. 30

Teaching the Literature
____ Reading the Selection   ❑ PE pp. 618–621

Thinking Through the Literature
____ Connect to the Literature
____ Think Critically   ❑ Reading and Critical Thinking Transparencies, T5
____ Extend Interpretations
____ Literary Analysis: Ballads

Choices and Challenges
Writing Options
____ Original Ballad
____ Points of Comparison

Activities and Explorations
____ Learned By Heart
____ Sorrowful Song
____ Ballads of Today

Inquiry and Research
____ Events in Birmingham

____ **Author Activity**

Copyright © McDougal Littell Inc.

Teaching Options (from Teacher's Edition)

Mini Lessons

Grammar

____ Introduction to Noun Clauses   ❑ Grammar Transparencies and Copymasters, C101

Informal Assessment

____ Identifying Theme

Assessment

____ Selection Test

____ Part Test

____ Test Generator

❑ Unit Four Resource Book: Selection Quiz, p. 117

❑ Formal Assessment: Unit Four, Part 1 Test, pp. 119–120

Homework Assignments

_____

_____

_____

_____

_____

Other Teaching Materials

_____

_____

_____

_____

_____

Copyright © McDougal Littell Inc.

Literary Interpretation

Writing Prompt
Write an interpretation of a literary work
in which you explain its meaning.

_____

Preparing

___ Introduction
___ Basics in a Box
___ Using the Graphic

❏ Writing Transparencies and Copymasters, T11, T20, C30

___ Analyzing a Student Model
"The Red Badge of Courage"

❏ Unit Four Resource Book: Student Models, pp. 38–43

Writing

___ **Prewriting**
Choosing a Literary Work
Planning the Literary Interpretation

❏ Unit Four Resource Book: Prewriting, p. 33

___ **Drafting**
Organizing the Draft

❏ Unit Four Resource Book: Drafting and Elaboration, p. 34

___ **Peer Review**
Ask Your Peer Reader

❏ Unit Four Resource Book: Peer Response Guide, pp. 35–36

___ **Revising**
Conclusions

❏ Unit Four Resource Book: Revising, Editing, and Proofreading, p. 37
❏ Unit Four Resource Book: Rubric for Evaluation, p. 44

___ **Editing and Proofreading**
Verb Tense

___ **Reflecting**

_____

┌─────────────────────────────────┐ ┌─────────────────────────────────┐
│ **Homework Assignments**   │ │ **Other Teaching Materials**   │
│   │ │   │
│ _____   │ │ _____   │
│ _____   │ │ _____   │
│ _____   │ │ _____   │
│ _____   │ │ _____   │
└─────────────────────────────────┘ └─────────────────────────────────┘

Copyright © McDougal Littell Inc.

The Indian and the Hundred Cows /
El indito de las cien vacas

Core Objectives
- Understand and appreciate a *cuento,* or a folk tale
- Identify characteristics of *cuentos*
- Determine the theme of a *cuento*

Integrating Skills

Grammar
- Independent and
  Subordinate Clauses

Vocabulary
- Using a Dictionary
  to Determine Usage

Preparing to Read
____ Connect to Your Life
____ Build Background
____ Focus Your Reading
Literary Analysis: Cuento   ❑ Unit Four Resource Book: Literary Analysis SkillBuilder, p. 49
Active Reading: Determining Theme   ❑ Unit Four Resource Book: Active Reading SkillBuilder, p. 48

Teaching the Literature
                                     ❑ PE pp. 638–644
____ Reading the Selection   ❑ Unit Four Resource Book: Summary, p. 47

Thinking Through the Literature
____ Connect to the Literature
____ Think Critically
____ Extend Interpretations
____ Literary Analysis: Cuento   ❑ Literary Analysis Transparencies, T24

Choices and Challenges

Writing Options
____ Sermon on Charity
____ Comic Tale

Activities and Explorations
____ Mural Art

Inquiry and Research
____ Translations from Spanish

Copyright © McDougal Littell Inc.

The Indian and the Hundred Cows /
El indito de las cien vacas

Teaching Options (from Teacher's Edition)

Mini Lessons

Vocabulary Strategy
____ Using a Dictionary to Determine Usage   ❏ Vocabulary Transparencies and Copymasters, C54

Grammar
____ Independent and Subordinate Clauses   ❏ Grammar Transparencies and Copymasters, C89

Speaking and Listening
____ Telling Stories

Informal Assessment
____ Making a Judgment

Assessment
____ Selection Quiz
____ Selection Test
____ Test Generator

❏ Unit Four Resource Book: Selection Quiz, p. 50
❏ Formal Assessment: Selection Test, p. 121

Homework Assignments

_____

_____

_____

_____

Other Teaching Materials

_____

_____

_____

_____

Copyright © McDougal Littell Inc.

High Horse's Courting *from* Black Elk Speaks   Pages 645–653

Core Objectives
- Appreciate a Sioux folk tale
- Understand and appreciate oral literature
- Identify author's purpose

Integrating Skills

Grammar
- Phrases and Clauses

Vocabulary
- Using Reference Materials

Preparing to Read
____ Connect to Your Life
____ Build Background
____ Focus Your Reading
    Literary Analysis: Oral Literature
    Active Reading: Identifying Author's Purpose

❑ Unit Four Resource Book: Literary Analysis SkillBuilder, p. 53
❑ Unit Four Resource Book: Active Reading SkillBuilder, p. 52

Teaching the Literature
____ Reading the Selection

❑ PE pp. 645–653
❑ Unit Four Resource Book: Summary, p. 51

Thinking Through the Literature
____ Connect to the Literature
____ Think Critically
____ Extend Interpretations
____ Literary Analysis: Oral Literature

❑ Reading and Critical Thinking Transparencies, T19

Choices and Challenges

Writing Options
____ Modernizing a Story

Activities and Explorations
____ Talk Show

Inquiry and Research
____ Sioux Culture

Copyright © McDougal Littell Inc.

High Horse's Courting *from* Black Elk Speaks

Teaching Options (from Teacher's Edition)

Mini Lessons

Vocabulary Strategy

___ Using Reference Materials: Specialized
Dictionaries

❑ Vocabulary Transparencies and Copymasters, C55

Grammar

___ Phrases and Clauses

❑ Grammar Transparencies and Copymasters, C90

Viewing and Representing

Art Appreciation

___ *Night Horse* by C. J. Wells

Cross Curricular Link

History

___ The Vanishing Frontier

Informal Assessment

___ Predicting Outcomes

Assessment

___ Selection Quiz

___ Selection Test

___ Test Generator

❑ Unit Four Resource Book: Selection Quiz, p. 54

❑ Formal Assessment: Selection Test, p. 123

Homework Assignments

_____

_____

_____

_____

_____

Other Teaching Materials

_____

_____

_____

_____

_____

Copyright © McDougal Littell Inc.

from The Autobiography of Mark Twain

Core Objectives
- Understand and appreciate an autobiography
- Identify and understand irony
- Predict events in an autobiography

Integrating Skills

Grammar
- Essential vs. Nonessential Clauses
- Punctuating Clauses in a Series

Vocabulary
- Using Context Clues
- Identifying Synonyms and Antonyms

Preparing to Read
____ Connect to Your Life
____ Build Background
____ Vocabulary Preview: Using Context Clues   ❑ Unit Four Resource Book: Words to Know SkillBuilder, p. 58
____ Focus Your Reading
      Literary Analysis: Irony   ❑ Unit Four Resource Book: Literary Analysis SkillBuilder, p. 57
      Active Reading: Predicting   ❑ Unit Four Resource Book: Active Reading SkillBuilder, p. 56

Teaching the Literature   ❑ PE pp. 658–668
____ Reading the Selection   ❑ Unit Four Resource Book: Summary, p. 55

Thinking Through the Literature
____ Connect to the Literature
____ Think Critically   ❑ Reading and Critical Thinking Transparencies, T2
____ Extend Interpretations
____ Literary Analysis: Irony

Choices and Challenges

Writing Options
____ Screenplay Script
____ Instruction Manual
____ Newspaper Report

Activities and Explorations
____ Stage Directions
____ Advertising Flyer

Inquiry and Research
____ Science

Vocabulary in Action
____ Assessment Practice

Copyright © McDougal Littell Inc.

from The Autobiography of Mark Twain

Teaching Options (from Teacher's Edition)
Mini Lessons

Preteaching Vocabulary
____ Using Context Clues

Vocabulary Strategy
____ Identifying Synonyms and Antonyms   ❑ Vocabulary Transparencies and Copymasters, C56

Grammar
____ Essential vs. Nonessential Clauses   ❑ Grammar Transparencies and Copymasters, T55, C91
____ Punctuating Clauses in a Series   ❑ Grammar Transparencies and Copymasters, C156

Speaking and Listening
____ Storytelling

Viewing and Representing
Art Appreciation
____ *Untitled*

Inquiry and Research
____ Using Indexes

Informal Assessment
____ Point of View

Assessment
____ Selection Quiz   ❑ Unit Four Resource Book: Selection Quiz, p. 59
____ Selection Test   ❑ Formal Assessment: Selection Test, pp. 125–126
____ Test Generator

Homework Assignments

_____
_____
_____
_____
_____

Other Teaching Materials

_____
_____
_____
_____
_____

Copyright © McDougal Littell Inc.

from Life on the Mississippi

Core Objectives
■ Appreciate a selection from a classic memoir
■ Appreciate and examine description
■ Visualize details in a memoir

Integrating Skills

Grammar   **Vocabulary**
■ Adjective Clauses   ■ Analogies
■ Commas with
  Names and Titles
■ Double Negatives

Preparing to Read
___ Connect to Your Life
___ Build Background
___ Focus Your Reading
    Literary Analysis: Description   ❏ Unit Four Resource Book: Literary Analysis SkillBuilder, p. 62
    Active Reading: Visualizing   ❏ Unit Four Resource Book: Active Reading SkillBuilder, p. 61

Teaching the Literature
                                            ❏ PE pp. 669–677
___ Reading the Selection   ❏ Unit Four Resource Book: Summary, p. 60

Thinking Through the Literature
___ Connect to the Literature
___ Think Critically   ❏ Reading and Critical Thinking Transparencies, T8
___ Extend Interpretations
___ Literary Analysis: Description

Choices and Challenges

Writing Options
___ Diary Entry
___ Magazine Article

Activities and Explorations
___ Occupational Outlook
___ Video Adaptation

Inquiry and Research
___ Geography

Copyright © McDougal Littell Inc.

from Life on the Mississippi

Teaching Options (from Teacher's Edition)

Mini Lessons

Vocabulary Strategy

___ Understanding Analogies

❏ Vocabulary Transparencies and Copymasters, C57

Grammar

___ Introductory Words for Adjective Clauses

❏ Grammar Transparencies and Copymasters, T44, C94

___ Commas in Names and Titles

❏ Grammar Transparencies and Copymasters, C150

Speaking and Listening

___ Persuading

Cross Curricular Link

Workplace

___ Starting a New Job

Informal Assessment

___ Story Extension

Assessment

___ Selection Quiz

❏ Unit Four Resource Book: Selection Quiz, p. 63

___ Selection Test

❏ Formal Assessment: Selection Test, pp. 127–128

___ Test Generator

Homework Assignments

_____

_____

_____

_____

_____

Other Teaching Materials

_____

_____

_____

_____

Copyright © McDougal Littell Inc.

Name _____   Date _____

The Notorious Jumping Frog of Calaveras County

Core Objectives

- Understand and appreciate a classic short story
- Identify characteristics of a tall tale
- Understand Twain's use of dialect

Integrating Skills

Grammar

- Use of *That* and *Which* in Adjective Clauses

Vocabulary

- Using Context Clues
- Applying Meanings of Root Words

Preparing to Read

____ Connect to Your Life
____ Build Background
____ Vocabulary Preview: Using Context Clues   ❏ Unit Four Resource Book: Words to Know SkillBuilder, p. 67
____ Focus Your Reading
     Literary Analysis: Tall Tale   ❏ Unit Four Resource Book: Literary Analysis SkillBuilder, p. 66
     Active Reading: Understanding Dialect   ❏ Unit Four Resource Book: Active Reading SkillBuilder, p. 65

Teaching the Literature

                                                ❏ PE pp. 679–687
____ Reading the Selection   ❏ Unit Four Resource Book: Summary, p. 64

Thinking Through the Literature

____ Connect to the Literature
____ Think Critically
____ Extend Interpretations
____ Literary Analysis: Tall Tale
____ Author's Style

Choices and Challenges

Writing Options

____ The Stranger's Tale
____ Local Storytelling
____ Dialects Today

Vocabulary in Action

____ Meaning Clues
____ Word Knowledge

____ **Author Study Project**

Copyright © McDougal Littell Inc.

The Notorious Jumping Frog of Calaveras County

Teaching Options (from Teacher's Edition)

Mini Lessons

Preteaching Vocabulary
____ Using Context Clues

Vocabulary Strategy
____ Applying Meanings of Root Words ❑ Vocabulary Transparencies and Copymasters, C58

Grammar
____ Use of *That* and *Which* in Adjective ❑ Grammar Transparencies and Copymasters, T44, C93
Clauses

Speaking and Listening
____ Telling a Humorous Anecdote

Viewing and Representing
____ Analyzing a Performance Review

Cross Curricular Link

Multicultural
____ Tall Tales of the 20th Century

Informal Assessment
____ Letter Writing

Assessment

____ Selection Quiz ❑ Unit Four Resource Book: Selection Quiz, p. 68
____ Selection Test ❑ Formal Assessment: Selection Test, pp. 129–130
____ Test Generator

Homework Assignments

_____

_____

_____

_____

_____

Other Teaching Materials

_____

_____

_____

_____

_____

Copyright © McDougal Littell Inc.

A Wagner Matinee

Core Objectives
- Understand and appreciate a short story
- Identify and understand setting
- Draw conclusions about character in a short story

Integrating Skills

Grammar	Vocabulary
■ Introductory Adverbial Clauses	■ Applying Meanings of Root Words
■ Punctuating Introductory Adverbial Clauses	

Preparing to Read
____ Connect to Your Life
____ Build Background
____ Vocabulary Preview: Applying Meanings   ❑ Unit Four Resource Book: Words to Know SkillBuilder, p. 72
    of Root Words
____ Focus Your Reading
    Literary Analysis: Setting   ❑ Unit Four Resource Book: Literary Analysis SkillBuilder, p. 71
    Active Reading: Drawing Conclusions   ❑ Unit Four Resource Book: Active Reading SkillBuilder, p. 70
       About Character

Teaching the Literature   ❑ PE pp. 688–699
____ Reading the Selection   ❑ Unit Four Resource Book: Summary, p. 69

Thinking Through the Literature
____ Connect to the Literature
____ Think Critically   ❑ Reading and Critical Thinking Transparencies, T1, T4, T39
____ Extend Interpretations
____ Literary Analysis: Setting   ❑ Literary Analysis Transparencies, T14

Choices and Challenges
Writing Options
____ Cause-and-Effect Analysis
____ Telegram from Boston
____ Interview: Personal Sacrifices

Activities and Explorations
____ Real Estate Ad
____ Opera Poster

Inquiry and Research
____ Music Appreciation

Vocabulary in Action
____ Context Clues

Author Activity
____ Willa Cather

Copyright © McDougal Littell Inc.

❑ Grammar Transparencies and Copymasters, C98
❑ Grammar Transparencies and Copymasters, C152

❑ Unit Four Resource Book: Selection Quiz, p. 73
❑ Formal Assessment: Selection Test, pp. 131–132

Homework Assignments

Other Teaching Materials

Copyright © McDougal Littell Inc.

The Legend of Gregorio Cortez

Core Objectives
- Appreciate a prose retelling of a traditional ballad
- Understand and appreciate a legend
- Make judgments about text

Integrating Skills

Grammar
- Introductory Words
  for Noun Clauses

Vocabulary
- Word History
- English from Spanish

Preparing to Read
____ Comparing Literature
____ Build Background
____ Focus Your Reading
     Literary Analysis: Legend   ❏ Unit Four Resource Book: Literary Analysis SkillBuilder, p. 76
     Active Reading: Making Judgments   ❏ Unit Four Resource Book: Active Reading SkillBuilder, p. 75
       About Text

Teaching the Literature
                                        ❏ PE pp. 702–719
____ Reading the Selection   ❏ Unit Four Resource Book: Summary, p. 74

Thinking Through the Literature
____ Connect to the Literature
____ Think Critically   ❏ Reading and Critical Thinking Transparencies, T5
____ Extend Interpretations
____ Literary Analysis: Legend   ❏ Literary Analysis Transparencies, T24

Choices and Challenges

Writing Options
____ Farewell Letter
____ Points of Comparison

Activities and Explorations
____ Map of the Setting
____ TV Newscast

Inquiry and Research
____ Colorful Folk Songs

Author Activity
____ The Storyteller's Voice

Copyright © McDougal Littell Inc.

The Legend of Gregorio Cortez

Teaching Options (from Teacher's Edition)

Mini Lessons

Vocabulary Strategy
____ Word History   ❑ Vocabulary Transparencies and Copymasters, C60
____ English from Spanish   ❑ Vocabulary Transparencies and Copymasters, C61

Grammar
____ Introductory Words for Noun Clauses   ❑ Grammar Transparencies and Copymasters, T44, C104

Viewing and Representing
Art Appreciation
____ *Chama Running Red* by John Sloan
____ *Cliffs, Beyond Abiquiu, Dry Waterfall* by Georgia O'Keefe

Cross Curricular Links

History
____ Texas Germans
____ Texas Rangers

Multicultural
____ Outlaw Heroes
____ Drawing from the Bible

Geography
____ Texas Geography

Government
____ Constitutional Law

Workplace Literacy
____ Writing Instructions

Informal Assessment
____ Character Clusters

Assessment
____ Selection Quiz   ❑ Unit Four Resource Book: Selection Quiz, p. 77
____ Selection Test   ❑ Formal Assessment: Selection Test, pp. 133–134
____ Part Test   ❑ Formal Assessment: Unit Four, Part 2 Test, pp. 135–136
____ Test Generator

Homework Assignments	**Other Teaching Materials**
_____	_____
_____	_____
_____	_____

Copyright © McDougal Littell Inc.

Storytelling

Writing Prompt:
Prepare a script or notes in which you plan
to tell a story. Then tell a story.

Preparing

____ Introduction

____ Basics in a Box

____ Using the Guidelines and Standards

____ Analyzing a Storytelling Script
A Storyteller in Action
"The Warrior Maiden"

❑ Unit Four Resource Book: Student Models, p. 84

Writing

____ **Prewriting**
Planning the Performance
Developing the Performance

❑ Unit Four Resource Book: Planning Your Performance, p. 79

____ **Drafting**
Developing your Script

____ **Practicing and Presenting**

❑ Unit Four Resource Book: Preparing, Practicing, and Presenting, p. 80

____ **Peer Review**
Ask Your Peer Reader

❑ Unit Four Resource Book: Peer Response Guide, pp. 81–82

____ **Refining Your Performance**
Evaluating Your Interpretive Choices

❑ Unit Four Resource Book: Refining, p. 83
❑ Unit Four Resource Book: Standards for Evaluation, p. 85

____ **Reflecting**

Copyright © McDougal Littell Inc.

Homework Assignments	**Other Teaching Materials**
_____	_____
_____	_____
_____	_____
_____	_____
_____	_____

Selected Poems by Emily Dickinson

Core Objectives

- Understand and appreciate representative poems by Emily Dickinson
- Identify and appreciate figurative language
- Apply strategies for reading poetry

Integrating Skills

Grammar	**Vocabulary**
■ Adjective and Adverb Clauses	■ Denotative and Connotative Meanings

Preparing to Read

____ Connect to Your Life

____ Build Background

____ Focus Your Reading

Literary Analysis: Figurative Language   ❏ Unit Five Resource Book: Literary Analysis SkillBuilder, p. 5

Active Reading: Strategies for Reading Poetry   ❏ Unit Five Resource Book: Active Reading SkillBuilder, p. 4

Teaching the Literature

____ Reading the Selection   ❏ PE pp. 750–762

Thinking Through the Literature

____ Connect to the Literature

____ Think Critically   ❏ Reading and Critical Thinking Transparencies, T50

____ Extend Interpretations

____ Literary Analysis: Figurative Language   ❏ Literary Analysis Transparencies, T13

Choices and Challenges

Writing Options

____ Mini Poem

____ Comparison Contrast Essay

Activities and Explorations

____ Illustrated Poem

____ Video Adaptation

Inquiry and Research

____ Historical Connection

Author Activity

____ Presenting a Poetry Slam

Copyright © McDougal Littell Inc.

Selected Poems by Emily Dickinson

Teaching Options (from Teacher's Edition)

Mini Lessons

Vocabulary Strategy

____ Denotative and Connotative Meanings ❑ Vocabulary Transparencies and Copymasters, C62

Grammar

____ Adjective and Adverb Clauses ❑ Grammar Transparencies and Copymasters, C100

Cross Curricular Link

Social Sciences

____ Women's Education in the 19th Century

Informal Assessment

____ Recognizing Poetic Form

____ Making Inferences

Assessment

____ Selection Test ❑ Formal Assessment: Selection Test, pp. 137–138

____ Test Generator

Homework Assignments

_____

_____

_____

_____

Other Teaching Materials

_____

_____

_____

_____

Copyright © McDougal Littell Inc.

The Yellow Wallpaper

Pages 765–781

Core Objectives

- Understand and appreciate a classic short story
- Examine first-person narrator in a short story
- Make inferences about the narrator

Integrating Skills

Grammar
- Subject-Verb Agreement
- Sentence Fragments

Vocabulary
- Using Context Clues
- Word Origins

Preparing to Read

____ Connect to Your Life
____ Build Background
____ Vocabulary Preview: Using Context Clues   ❑ Unit Five Resource Book: Words to Know SkillBuilder, p. 9
____ Focus Your Reading
    Literary Analysis: First-Person Narrator   ❑ Unit Five Resource Book: Literary Analysis SkillBuilder, p. 8
    Active Reading: Making Inferences About   ❑ Unit Five Resource Book: Active Reading SkillBuilder, p. 7
      the Narrator

Teaching the Literature

    ❑ PE pp. 765–781
____ Reading the Selection   ❑ Unit Five Resource Book: Summary, p. 6

Thinking Through the Literature

____ Connect to the Literature
____ Think Critically   ❑ Reading and Critical Thinking Transparencies, T7
____ Extend Interpretations
____ Literary Analysis: First-Person Narrator   ❑ Literary Analysis Transparencies, T14

Choices and Challenges

Writing Options
____ Advertising Copy
____ Letter to Editor
____ Extend the Story

Activities and Explorations
____ Dramatic Scene
____ Wallpaper Design
____ Top Story

Inquiry and Research
____ Depression

Vocabulary in Action
____ Meaning Clues

Copyright © McDougal Littell Inc.

Teaching Options (from Teacher's Edition)

Mini Lessons

Preteaching Vocabulary
____ Using Context Clues

Vocabulary Strategy
____ Word Origins ❑ Vocabulary Transparencies and Copymasters, C63

Grammar
____ Subject-Verb Agreement ❑ Grammar Transparencies and Copymasters, T47, C108
____ Sentence Fragments ❑ Grammar Transparencies and Copymasters, C124

Speaking and Listening
____ Dramatic Reading
____ Role Playing

Viewing and Representing
Art Appreciation
____ *A Woman Sewing in an Interior*
by Wilhelm Hammershøi
____ *Stairway* by Edward Hopper

Cross Curricular Link

Psychology
____ Depression

Informal Assessment

____ Story Log
____ Sentence Completion

Assessment

____ Selection Quiz ❑ Unit Five Resource Book: Selection Quiz, p. 10
____ Selection Test ❑ Formal Assessment: Selection Test, pp. 139–140
____ Test Generator

Homework Assignments

_____
_____
_____
_____
_____

Other Teaching Materials

_____
_____
_____
_____
_____

Copyright © McDougal Littell Inc.

The Story of an Hour

Core Objectives
- Understand and appreciate a short story
- Identify and appreciate plot and conflict
- Use clues in the story to make predictions

Integrating Skills

Grammar
- Reviewing Complete Sentences

Vocabulary
- Using Reference Sources

Preparing to Read
____ Connect to Your Life
____ Build Background
____ Focus Your Reading
      Literary Analysis: Plot   ❏ Unit Five Resource Book: Literary Analysis SkillBuilder, p. 13
      Active Reading: Predicting   ❏ Unit Five Resource Book: Active Reading SkillBuilder, p. 12

Teaching the Literature
                                 ❏ PE pp. 783–787
____ Reading the Selection   ❏ Unit Five Resource Book: Summary, p. 11

Thinking Through the Literature
____ Connect to the Literature
____ Think Critically   ❏ Reading and Critical Thinking Transparencies, T2
____ Extend Interpretations
____ Literary Analysis: Plot and Surprise Ending

Choices and Challenges

Writing Options
____ Husband's Monologue
____ Wife's Epitaph
____ Different Ending
____ Essay About Marriage

Activities and Explorations
____ Story and Video

Inquiry and Research
____ Depression

Copyright © McDougal Littell Inc.

Teaching Options (from Teacher's Edition)

Mini Lessons

Vocabulary Strategy

____ Using Reference Sources

❏ Vocabulary Transparencies and Copymasters, C64

Grammar

____ Reviewing Complete Sentences

❏ Grammar Transparencies and Copymasters, T42, C73

Informal Assessment

____ Storyboard

Assessment

____ Selection Quiz

____ Selection Test

____ Test Generator

❏ Unit Five Resource Book: Selection Quiz, p. 14

❏ Formal Assessment: Selection Test, pp. 141–142

Homework Assignments

_____

_____

_____

_____

Other Teaching Materials

_____

_____

_____

_____

Copyright © McDougal Littell Inc.

Name _____ Date _____

Seventeen Syllables

Core Objectives
- Appreciate a Japanese-American short story
- Examine a coming-of-age story
- Understand conflict

Integrating Skills

Grammar
- Adverb Clauses
- Semicolons and Conjunctive Adverbs

Vocabulary
- Using Context Clues
- Idioms

Preparing to Read
____ Comparing Literature
____ Build Background
____ Vocabulary Preview: Using Context Clues: ❑ Unit Five Resource Book: Words to Know SkillBuilder, p. 18
Synonyms
____ Focus Your Reading
Literary Analysis: Coming-of-Age Story ❑ Unit Five Resource Book: Literary Analysis SkillBuilder, p. 17
Active Reading: Understanding Conflicts ❑ Unit Five Resource Book: Active Reading SkillBuilder, p. 16

Teaching the Literature
❑ PE pp. 788–801
____ Reading the Selection ❑ Unit Five Resource Book: Summary, p. 15

Thinking Through the Literature
____ Connect to the Literature
____ Think Critically
____ Extend Interpretations
____ Literary Analysis: Coming-of-Age Story

Choices and Challenges
Writing Options
____ Points of Comparison
____ Character Sketch

Vocabulary in Action
____ Context Clues

Copyright © McDougal Littell Inc.

Seventeen Syllables

Teaching Options (from Teacher's Edition)

Mini Lessons

Preteaching Vocabulary

____ Using Context Clues: Synonyms

Vocabulary Strategy

____ Using Context to Understand Idioms ❑ Vocabulary Transparencies and Copymasters, C65

Grammar

____ Adverb Clauses: Subordinating Clauses ❑ Grammar Transparencies and Copymasters, C97

____ Semicolons and Conjunctive Adverbs ❑ Grammar Transparencies and Copymasters, C157

Speaking and Listening

____ Problem Solving by Role-Playing

Viewing and Representing

Art Appreciation

____ *Consolation* by Ruth Gikow

____ *Japanese American Family in the 1930s* by Russell Lee

____ *Returning Sails to Gyotoku* by Ichiryusai Hiroshige

Cross Curricular Link

Workplace

____ Reading Maps

Informal Assessment

____ Arranging Events in Sequence

____ Self-Assessment

Assessment

____ Selection Quiz ❑ Unit Five Resource Book: Selection Quiz, p. 19

____ Selection Test ❑ Formal Assessment: Selection Test, pp. 143–144

____ Test Generator

Homework Assignments

_____

_____

_____

_____

Other Teaching Materials

_____

_____

_____

_____

Copyright © McDougal Littell Inc.

Core Objectives
- Understand and appreciate a modern poem
- Identify and appreciate imagery
- Visualize the images in a poem

Integrating Skills

Grammar
- Adverb Clauses

Vocabulary
- Researching Word Origins

Preparing to Read
____ Comparing Literature
____ Build Background
____ Focus Your Reading
      Literary Analysis: Imagery   ❑ Unit Five Resource Book: Literary Analysis SkillBuilder, p. 21
      Active Reading: Visualizing   ❑ Unit Five Resource Book: Active Reading SkillBuilder, p. 20

Teaching the Literature
____ Reading the Selection   ❑ PE pp. 802–805

Thinking Through the Literature
____ Connect to the Literature
____ Think Critically   ❑ Reading and Critical Thinking Transparencies, T8
____ Extend Interpretations
____ Literary Analysis: Imagery

Choices and Challenges
Writing Options
____ Points of Comparison
____ Rosie's Diary Entry
____ Write a Review

Activities and Explorations
____ Sketch
____ Oral Interpretation

Copyright © McDougal Littell Inc.

Teaching Options (from Teacher's Edition)

Mini Lessons

Vocabulary Strategy

___ Researching Word Origins

❑ Vocabulary Transparencies and Copymasters, C66

Grammar

___ Adverb Clauses

Assessment

___ Selection Test

___ Test Generator

❑ Formal Assessment: Selection Test, pp. 145–146

Homework Assignments

_____

_____

_____

_____

_____

Other Teaching Materials

_____

_____

_____

_____

_____

Copyright © McDougal Littell Inc.

I Stand Here Ironing

Core Objectives

- Understand and appreciate a short story
- Understand interior monologue
- Make judgments about character

Integrating Skills

Grammar	Vocabulary
■ Adverbial Clauses with *Because*	■ Using Context Clues ■ Homonyms

Preparing to Read

____ Comparing Literature

____ Build Background

____ Vocabulary Preview: Using Context Clues　　❑ Unit Five Resource Book: Words to Know SkillBuilder, p. 25

____ Focus Your Reading

　　　Literary Analysis: Interior Monologue　　❑ Unit Five Resource Book: Literary Analysis SkillBuilder, p. 24

　　　Active Reading: Making Judgments　　　❑ Unit Five Resource Book: Active Reading SkillBuilder, p. 23
　　　　About Character

Teaching the Literature

　　　　　　　　　　　　　　　　　　　　❑ PE pp. 806–817

____ Reading the Selection　　　　　　　　❑ Unit Five Resource Book: Summary, p. 22

Thinking Through the Literature

____ Connect to the Literature

____ Think Critically　　　　　　　　　　　❑ Reading and Critical Thinking Transparencies, T5, T15

____ Extend Interpretations

____ Literary Analysis: Interior Monologue

Choices and Challenges

Writing Options

____ Points of Comparison

____ Story Sequel

____ Response to Relationships

____ Emily's Interview

Activities and Explorations

____ Guidelines for Parents

____ Informal Discussion

____ Role Play

____ **Art Connection**

____ **Inquiry and Research**

____ Sibling Rivalry

____ Oral History

Copyright © McDougal Littell Inc.

Choices and Challenges (continued)

Vocabulary in Action
____ Meaning Clues

Teaching Options (from Teacher's Edition)

Mini Lessons

Preteaching Vocabulary
____ Using Context Clues ❏ Vocabulary Transparencies and Copymasters, C67

Vocabulary Strategy
____ Homonyms

Grammar
____ Adverbial Clauses with *Because* ❏ Grammar Transparencies and Copymasters, C99

Speaking and Listening
____ Interviews

Viewing and Representing
Art Appreciation
____ *Girl Skipping Rope* by Ben Shahn
____ *The Brown Sweater* by Raphael Soyer

Cross Curricular Link

History
____ Working Women During the Depression

Informal Assessment
____ Point of View
____ Choosing the Best Summary

Assessment
____ Selection Quiz ❏ Unit Five Resource Book: Selection Quiz, p. 26
____ Selection Test ❏ Formal Assessment: Selection Test, pp. 147–148
____ Part Test ❏ Formal Assessment: Unit Five, Part 1 Test, pp. 149–150
____ Test Generator

Homework Assignments
_____
_____
_____
_____
_____

Other Teaching Materials
_____
_____
_____
_____
_____

Copyright © McDougal Littell Inc.

Chicago / Lucinda Matlock

Core Objectives
- Appreciate two classic poems
- Identify and examine tone
- Synthesize details in poetry

Integrating Skills

Grammar
- Noun Clauses

Vocabulary
- Denotation and Connotation

Preparing to Read
____ Connect to Your Life
____ Build Background
____ Focus Your Reading

Literary Analysis: Tone   ❑ Unit Five Resource Book: Literary Analysis SkillBuilder, p. 29
Active Reading: Synthesizing Details   ❑ Unit Five Resource Book: Active Reading SkillBuilder, p. 28

Teaching the Literature
____ Reading the Selection   ❑ PE pp. 824–829

Thinking Through the Literature
____ Connect to the Literature
____ Think Critically   ❑ Reading and Critical Thinking Transparencies, T16
____ Extend Interpretations
____ Literary Analysis: Tone   ❑ Literary Analysis Transparencies, T19

Choices and Challenges
Writing Options
____ Hometown Poems
____ Comparison-Contrast Essay

Copyright © McDougal Littell Inc.

Chicago / Lucinda Matlock

Teaching Options (from Teacher's Edition)

Mini Lessons

Vocabulary Strategy

____ Discriminating Between Connotative and Denotative Meaning

❏ Vocabulary Transparencies and Copymasters, C68

Grammar

____ Noun Clauses

❏ Grammar Transparencies and Copymasters, C102

Viewing and Representing

Art Appreciation

____ *City Building* and *Country Dance* by Thomas Hart Benton

Assessment

____ Selection Test

____ Test Generator

❏ Formal Assessment: Selection Test, pp. 151–152

Homework Assignments

_____

_____

_____

_____

_____

Other Teaching Materials

_____

_____

_____

_____

_____

Copyright © McDougal Littell Inc.

Richard Cory / Miniver Cheevy

Core Objectives
- Appreciate two narrative poems
- Understand characterization in narrative poetry
- Evaluate character in poetry

Integrating Skills
Grammar	Vocabulary
■ Noun Clauses	■ Idioms

Preparing to Read
____ Connect to Your Life
____ Build Background
____ Focus Your Reading
    Literary Analysis: Characterization in   ❑ Unit Five Resource Book: Literary Analysis SkillBuilder, p. 31
       Narrative Poetry
    Active Reading: Evaluating Character   ❑ Unit Five Resource Book: Active Reading SkillBuilder, p. 30

Teaching the Literature
____ Reading the Selection   ❑ PE pp. 830–834

Thinking Through the Literature
____ Connect to the Literature
____ Think Critically   ❑ Reading and Critical Thinking Transparencies, T15
____ Extend Interpretations
____ Literary Analysis: Characterization in Narrative   ❑ Literary Analysis Transparencies, T6
    Poetry

Choices and Challenges
Writing Options
____ Miniver's Monologue
____ Farewell Note
____ Interview Questions

Activities and Explorations
____ Musical Adaptation
Author Activities

Copyright © McDougal Littell Inc.

Richard Cory / Miniver Cheevy

Teaching Options (from Teacher's Edition)

Mini Lessons

Vocabulary Strategy

____ Rely on Context to Determine Meanings of Idioms

❑ Vocabulary Transparencies and Copymasters, C69

Grammar

____ Noun Clause

❑ Grammar Transparencies and Copymasters, C102

Informal Assessment

____ Identifying the Best Summary

Assessment

____ Selection Test

____ Test Generator

❑ Formal Assessment: Selection Test, pp. 153–154

Homework Assignments

_____

_____

_____

_____

_____

Other Teaching Materials

_____

_____

_____

_____

Copyright © McDougal Littell Inc.

We Wear the Mask / Sympathy

Core Objectives
- Understand and appreciate two poems
- Identify and examine symbol in poetry
- Interpret symbols in poetry

Integrating Skills

Grammar   **Vocabulary**
- Appositive Clauses   ■ Connotation

Preparing to Read
____ Connect to Your Life
____ Build Background
____ Focus Your Reading
    Literary Analysis: Symbols   ❑ Unit Five Resource Book: Literary Analysis SkillBuilder, p. 33
    Active Reading: Interpreting Symbols   ❑ Unit Five Resource Book: Active Reading SkillBuilder, p. 32

Teaching the Literature
____ Reading the Selection   ❑ PE pp. 835–839

Thinking Through the Literature
____ Connect to the Literature
____ Think Critically
____ Extend Interpretations
____ Literary Analysis: Symbols   ❑ Literary Analysis Transparencies, T19

Choices and Challenges
Writing Options
____ Narrative Sequel
____ Lyrics of a Songbird

Activities and Explorations
____ Personal Mask
____ Political Cartoon

____ **Author Activity**

Copyright © McDougal Littell Inc.

We Wear the Mask / Sympathy

Teaching Options (from Teacher's Edition)

Mini Lessons

Vocabulary Strategy

____ Interpret Connotative Power of Words ❏ Vocabulary Transparencies and Copymasters, C70

Grammar

____ Appositive Clauses ❏ Grammar Transparencies and Copymasters, C105

Assessment

____ Selection Test

____ Test Generator ❏ Formal Assessment: Selection Test, pp. 155–156

Homework Assignments

_____

_____

_____

_____

_____

Other Teaching Materials

_____

_____

_____

_____

_____

Copyright © McDougal Littell Inc.

Winter Dreams

Core Objectives
- Understand and appreciate a short story
- Analyze characters
- Evaluate character

Integrating Skills

Grammar
- Punctuation: Semicolons
- Noun Clauses

Vocabulary
- Using Context Clues
- Applying Meanings of Root Words

Preparing to Read
____ Connect to Your Life
____ Build Background
____ Vocabulary Preview: Using Context Clues   ❑ Unit Five Resource Book: Words to Know SkillBuilder, p. 37
____ Focus Your Reading
      Literary Analysis: Characters   ❑ Unit Five Resource Book: Literary Analysis SkillBuilder, p. 36
      Active Reading: Evaluating Character   ❑ Unit Five Resource Book: Active Reading SkillBuilder, p. 35

Teaching the Literature   ❑ PE pp. 840–862
____ Reading the Selection   ❑ Unit Five Resource Book: Summary, p. 34

Thinking Through the Literature
____ Connect to the Literature
____ Think Critically   ❑ Reading and Critical Thinking Transparencies, T55
____ Extend Interpretations
____ Literary Analysis: Characters   ❑ Literary Analysis Transparencies, T6

Choices and Challenges
Writing Options
____ Psychological Evaluation
____ Dexter's Résumé
____ Personal Lecture

Activities and Explorations
____ Illustrated Calendar

Inquiry and Research
____ Clothing Styles

Art Connection

Vocabulary in Action
____ Synonyms

Copyright © McDougal Littell Inc.

Teaching Options (from Teacher's Edition)

Mini Lessons

Preteaching Vocabulary
____ Using Context Clues

Vocabulary Strategy
____ Applying Meanings of Root Words   ❏ Vocabulary Transparencies and Copymasters, C71

Grammar
____ Punctuation: Semicolons   ❏ Grammar Transparencies and Copymasters, C158
____ Noun Clauses   ❏ Grammar Transparencies and Copymasters, C103

Speaking and Listening
____ Historical Recordings
____ Dramatic Reading

Viewing and Representing
Art Appreciation
____ *Autoportrait* by Tamara de Lempicka
____ *The Shelton with Sunspots* by Georgia O'Keefe

Assessment Preparation
____ Point of View
____ Alternative Ending

Inquiry and Research
____ Using Indexes

Cross Curricular Links

Music
____ Roots of Jazz

History
____ Women After World War I

Social Studies
____ The Aftermath of World War I

Informal Assessment
____ Point of View
____ Alternative Ending

Assessment
____ Selection Quiz   ❏ Unit Five Resource Book: Selection Quiz, p. 38
____ Selection Test   ❏ Formal Assessment: Selection Test, pp. 157–158
____ Test Generator

Homework Assignments	**Other Teaching Materials**

Copyright © McDougal Littell Inc.

America and I

Core Objectives
- Understand and appreciate a short story
- Identify the elements of style that create voice
- Understand analogies

Integrating Skills

Grammar
- Commas: Introductory Words
- Noun Clauses: Common Introductory Words

Vocabulary
- Using Context Clues
- Suffixes and Root Words

Preparing to Read
____ Connect to Your Life
____ Vocabulary Preview: Using Context Clues   ❑ Unit Five Resource Book: Words to Know SkillBuilder, p. 42
____ Focus Your Reading
    Literary Analysis: Voice   ❑ Unit Five Resource Book: Literary Analysis SkillBuilder, p. 41
    Active Reading: Understanding Analogies   ❑ Unit Five Resource Book: Active Reading SkillBuilder, p. 40

Teaching the Literature
❑ PE pp. 863–874
____ Reading the Selection   ❑ Unit Five Resource Book: Summary, p. 39

Thinking Through the Literature
____ Connect to the Literature
____ Think Critically   ❑ Reading and Critical Thinking Transparencies, T15
____ Extend Interpretations
____ Literary Analysis: Voice   ❑ Literary Analysis Transparencies, T23

Choices and Challenges

Writing Options
____ Tips for Newcomers
____ Letter to Russia
____ Looking Back: A Memoir

Vocabulary in Action
____ Context Clues

Copyright © McDougal Littell Inc.

America and I

Teaching Options (from Teacher's Edition)

Mini Lessons

Preteaching Vocabulary
____ Using Context Clues

Vocabulary Strategy
____ Suffixes and Root Words

Grammar
____ Commas: Introductory Words
____ Noun Clauses: Common Introductory Words

Speaking and Listening
____ Yiddish Words

Viewing and Representing
Art Appreciation
____ Photographs

❏ Vocabulary Transparencies and Copymasters, C72

❏ Grammar Transparencies and Copymasters, C104
❏ Grammar Transparencies and Copymasters, C153

Cross Curricular Links

History
____ Triangle Shirtwaist Company

Workplace
____ Reaching a Compromise

Informal Assessment
____ Choosing the Best Summary

Assessment
____ Selection Quiz
____ Selection Test
____ Test Generator

❏ Unit Five Resource Book: Selection Quiz, p. 43
❏ Formal Assessment: Selection Test, pp. 159–160

Homework Assignments

_____
_____
_____
_____
_____

Other Teaching Materials

_____
_____
_____
_____
_____

Copyright © McDougal Littell Inc.

In the American Society

Core Objectives
- Appreciate a contemporary short story
- Identify and examine structure
- Make inferences about motivations

Integrating Skills

Grammar
- Noun Clauses

Vocabulary
- Context Clues
- Word History

Preparing to Read
___ Build Background
___ Vocabulary Preview: Using Context Clues   ❏ Unit Five Resource Book: Words to Know SkillBuilder, p. 47
___ Focus Your Reading
    Literary Analysis: Structure   ❏ Unit Five Resource Book: Literary Analysis SkillBuilder, p. 46
    Active Reading: Making Inferences   ❏ Unit Five Resource Book: Active Reading SkillBuilder, p. 45
      About Motivation

Teaching the Literature   ❏ PE pp. 877–893
___ Reading the Selection   ❏ Unit Five Resource Book: Summary, p. 44

Thinking Through the Literature
___ Connect to the Literature
___ Think Critically   ❏ Reading and Critical Thinking Transparencies, T7
___ Extend Interpretations
___ Literary Analysis: Structure

Choices and Challenges

Writing Options
___ Points of Comparison
___ Argument About Assimilation
___ Critical Review

Vocabulary in Action
___ Assessment Practice
___ Meaning Clues

Copyright © McDougal Littell Inc.

In the American Society

Teaching Options (from Teacher's Edition)

Mini Lessons

Preteaching Vocabulary
____ Using Context Clues

Vocabulary Strategy
____ Word History

❑ Vocabulary Transparencies and Copymasters, C73

Grammar
____ Introductory Words for Noun Clauses—
Who and *Whom*

❑ Grammar Transparencies and Copymasters, C106

Speaking and Listening
____ Mandarin

Viewing and Representing
Art Appreciation
____ *Diner Interior with Coffee Urns* by Ralph Goings
____ *The Splash* by David Hockney

Cross Curricular Link
____ Religions in China

Workplace Links
____ Participating as a Member of a Team
____ Government
____ Immigration Law

Informal Assessment
____ Missing Chapter
____ Narrator's Voice

Assessment
____ Selection Quiz
____ Selection Test
____ Test Generator

❑ Unit Five Resource Book: Selection Quiz, p. 48
❑ Formal Assessment: Selection Test, pp. 161–162

Homework Assignments

_____
_____
_____
_____
_____

Other Teaching Materials

_____
_____
_____
_____

Copyright © McDougal Littell Inc.

Defining the Grateful Gesture / Refugee Ship   Pages 894–899

Core Objectives
- Understand and appreciate two contemporary poems
- Understand how theme and title are related
- Draw conclusions about theme

Integrating Skills
Grammar   **Vocabulary**
- Pronouns in   ■ Analogies
  Comparison

Preparing to Read
____ Comparing Literature
____ Build Background
____ Focus Your Reading
    Literary Analysis: Theme and Title   ❑ Unit Five Resource Book: Literary Analysis SkillBuilder, p. 50
    Active Reading: Drawing Conclusions   ❑ Unit Five Resource Book: Active Reading SkillBuilder, p. 49
      About Theme

Teaching the Literature
____ Reading the Selection   ❑ PE pp. 894–899

Thinking Through the Literature
____ Connect to the Literature
____ Think Critically   ❑ Reading and Critical Thinking Transparencies, T4, T57
____ Extend Interpretations
____ Literary Analysis: Theme and Title

Choices and Challenges
Writing Options
____ Points of Comparison
____ Review of Sapia's Language

Activities and Explorations
____ Musical Adaptation

Copyright © McDougal Littell Inc.

Defining the Grateful Gesture / Refugee Ship

Teaching Options (from Teacher's Edition)

Mini Lessons

Vocabulary Strategy

____ Understanding Analogies

❑ Vocabulary Transparencies and Copymasters, C74

Grammar

____ Pronouns in Comparison

❑ Grammar Transparencies and Copymasters, C126

Viewing and Representing

Art Appreciation

____ *Analogia IV* by Victor Grippo

Informal Assessment

____ Open-Ended Reading Items

Assessment

____ Selection Test

❑ Unit Five Resource Book: Selection Test, pp. 163–164

____ Part Test

❑ Formal Assessment: Unit Five Part 2 Test, pp. 165–166

____ Test Generator

Homework Assignments

_____

_____

_____

_____

Other Teaching Materials

_____

_____

_____

_____

Copyright © McDougal Littell Inc.

Comparison-and-Contrast Essay

Writing Prompt
Write a comparison-and-contrast essay in which
you explore the similarities and differences
between two or more subjects that interest you.

Preparing
____ Introduction
____ Basics in a Box
____ Using the Graphic

❑ Writing Transparencies and Copymasters, T11, T20, C31, C32

____ Analyzing a Student Model
"Antigua: Almost Paradise"

❑ Unit Five Resource Book: Student Models, pp. 57–62

Writing
____ Prewriting
Choosing a Subject
Planning the Comparison-and-Contrast Essay

❑ Unit Five Resource Book: Prewriting, p. 52

____ Drafting
Organizing the Draft

❑ Unit Five Resource Book: Drafting and Elaboration, p. 53

____ Peer Review
Ask Your Peer Reader

❑ Unit Five Resource Book: Peer Response Guide, pp. 54–55

____ Revising
Parallel Construction

❑ Unit Five Resource Book: Revising, Editing, and Proofreading, p. 56
❑ Unit Five Resource Book: Rubric for Evaluation, p. 63

____ Editing and Proofreading
Modifiers

____ Reflecting

Homework Assignments
_____
_____
_____
_____
_____

Other Teaching Materials
_____
_____
_____
_____
_____

Copyright © McDougal Littell Inc.

Selected Poems by Langston Hughes

Core Objectives
- Understand and appreciate representative poems by Langston Hughes
- Identify and appreciate mood
- Detect rhythm in poetry

Integrating Skills

Grammar
- Varying Sentence Structure

Vocabulary
- Understanding Syllabic Marks

Preparing to Read
____ Connect to Your Life
____ Build Background
____ Focus Your Reading
    Literary Analysis: Mood   ❑ Unit Six Resource Book: Literary Analysis SkillBuilder, p. 5
    Active Reading: Detecting Rhythm in Poetry   ❑ Unit Six Resource Book: Active Reading SkillBuilder, p. 4

Teaching the Literature
____ Reading the Selection   ❑ PE pp. 924–929

Thinking Through the Literature
____ Connect to the Literature
____ Think Critically
____ Extend Interpretations
____ Literary Analysis: Mood   ❑ Literary Analysis Transparencies, T18

Choices and Challenges

Writing Options
____ Congratulatory Letter
____ Musical Poem
____ Compare-Contrast Essay

Activities and Explorations
____ Oral Readings
____ Poem Illustration
____ Map of Harlem
____ Blues Adaptation

Inquiry and Research
____ The Blues

Copyright © McDougal Littell Inc.

Teaching Options

Mini Lessons

Vocabulary Strategy
____ Understanding Syllabic Marks   ❏ Vocabulary Transparencies and Copymasters, C75

Grammar
____ Varying Sentence Structure   ❏ Grammar Transparencies and Copymasters, C164

Viewing and Representing
Art Appreciation
____ *Black Manhattan* by Romare Bearden _____

Informal Assessment
____ Oral Reading _____

Assessment
____ Selection Test   ❏ Formal Assessment: Selection Test, pp. 167–168
____ Test Generator

Homework Assignments	Other Teaching Materials
_____	_____
_____	_____
_____	_____
_____	_____
_____	_____

Copyright © McDougal Littell Inc.

When the Negro Was in Vogue

Core Objectives

- Understand and appreciate an essay
- Identify tone
- Draw conclusions about author's perspective

Integrating Skills

Grammar

- Adverbial Elements

Vocabulary

- Using Context to Build Vocabulary

Preparing to Read

____ Connect to Your Life

____ Build Background

____ Focus Your Reading

____ Literary Analysis: Tone   ❑ Unit Six Resource Book: Literary Analysis SkillBuilder, p. 7

____ Active Reading: Drawing Conclusions   ❑ Unit Six Resource Book: Active Reading SkillBuilder, p. 6
      About Author's Perspective

Teaching the Literature

____ Reading the Selection   ❑ PE pp. 932–939

Thinking Through the Literature

____ Connect to the Literature

____ Think Critically   ❑ Reading and Critical Thinking Transparencies, T4, T22

____ Extend Interpretations

____ Literary Analysis: Tone   ❑ Literary Analysis Transparencies, T19

Choices and Challenges

Writing Options

____ Autobiographical Essay

____ Documentary Plan

Activities and Explorations

____ Music of the 1920s

____ Do the Lindy

Inquiry and Research

____ The Harlem Renaissance

____ **Author Study Project**

Copyright © McDougal Littell Inc.

When the Negro Was in Vogue

Teaching Options (from Teacher's Edition)

Mini Lessons

Vocabulary Strategy
____ Using Context to Build Vocabulary

❏ Vocabulary Transparencies and Copymasters, C76

Grammar
____ Adverbial Elements

❏ Grammar Transparencies and Copymasters, C140

Speaking and Listening
____ Nonverbal Communication

Cross Curricular Link

Music
____ Recordings of Blues and Jazz

Informal Assessment
____ Summary

Assessment
____ Selection Test
____ Test Generator

❏ Formal Assessment: Selection Test, pp. 169–170

Homework Assignments

_____

_____

_____

_____

_____

Other Teaching Materials

_____

_____

_____

_____

Copyright © McDougal Littell Inc.

My City / Any Human to Another

Core Objectives
- Understand and appreciate two sonnets
- Determine major ideas in a poem

Integrating Skills

Grammar
- Modifiers: Comparative and Superlative

Vocabulary
- Figurative Language

Preparing to Read
___ Connect to Your Life
___ Build Background
___ Focus Your Reading
    Literary Analysis: Sonnet   ❏ Unit Six Resource Book: Literary Analysis SkillBuilder, p. 9
    Active Reading: Determining Major Ideas in   ❏ Unit Six Resource Book: Active Reading SkillBuilder, p. 8
    a Poem

Teaching the Literature
___ Reading the Selection   ❏ PE pp. 940–944

Thinking Through the Literature
___ Connect to the Literature
___ Think Critically   ❏ Reading and Critical Thinking Transparencies, T12, T48
___ Extend Interpretations
___ Literary Analysis: Sonnet   ❏ Literary Analysis Transparencies, T11

Choices and Challenges

Writing Options
___ Slogan About New York
___ Write a Review

Inquiry and Research
___ Art

Copyright © McDougal Littell Inc.

My City / Any Human to Another

Teaching Options (from Teacher's Edition)

Mini Lessons

Vocabulary Strategy
____ Figurative Language

❑ Vocabulary Transparencies and Copymasters, C77

Grammar
____ Modifiers: Comparative and Superlative

❑ Grammar Transparencies and Copymasters, C132

Speaking and Listening
____ Reading Poetry

Assessment
____ Selection Test
____ Test Generator

❑ Formal Assessment: Selection Test, pp. 171–172

Homework Assignments
_____
_____
_____
_____
_____

Other Teaching Materials
_____
_____
_____
_____
_____

Copyright © McDougal Littell Inc.

If We Must Die / A Black Man Talks of Reaping   Pages 945–949

Core Objectives
- Understand and appreciate two poems
- Identify and examine extended metaphor
- Distinguish figurative and literal meaning

Integrating Skills

Grammar
- Modifiers

Vocabulary
- Prefixes

Preparing to Read
____ Connect to Your Life
____ Build Background
____ Focus Your Reading
    Literary Analysis: Extended Metaphor   ❏ Unit Six Resource Book: Literary Analysis SkillBuilder, p. 11
    Active Reading: Distinguishing Figurative and   ❏ Unit Six Resource Book: Active Reading SkillBuilder, p. 10
       Literal Meaning

Teaching the Literature
____ Reading the Selection   ❏ PE pp. 945–949

Thinking Through the Literature
____ Connect to the Literature
____ Think Critically   ❏ Reading and Critical Thinking Transparencies, T23, T56
____ Extend Interpretations
____ Literary Analysis: Extended Metaphor

Choices and Challenges

Writing Options
____ Problem-Solution Essay
____ Write a Sonnet

Activities and Explorations
____ Activist Poster

Copyright © McDougal Littell Inc.

If We Must Die / A Black Man Talks of Reaping

Teaching Options (from Teacher's Edition)

Mini Lessons

Vocabulary Strategy

____ Prefixes *In-* and *Out-* ❑ Vocabulary Transparencies and Copymasters, C78

Grammar

____ Modifiers: Use of *-er* ❑ Grammar Transparencies and Copymasters, C135

____ *Informal Assessment*

Assessment

____ Selection Test ❑ Formal Assessment: Selection Test, pp. 173–174

____ Test Generator

Homework Assignments

_____

_____

_____

_____

Other Teaching Materials

_____

_____

_____

_____

Copyright © McDougal Littell Inc.

How It Feels to Be Colored Me

Core Objectives
- Understand and appreciate an autobiographical essay
- Draw conclusions about author's purpose

Integrating Skills

Grammar	Vocabulary
■ Modifiers: Distinguishing *Those* from *Them*	■ Using Context Clues ■ Using Context Clues with Figurative Language

Preparing to Read
____ Connect to Your Life
____ Build Background
____ Vocabulary Preview: Using Context Clues ❏ Unit Six Resource Book: Words to Know SkillBuilder, p. 15
____ Focus Your Reading
    Literary Analysis: Autobiographical Essay ❏ Unit Six Resource Book: Literary Analysis SkillBuilder, p. 14
    Active Reading: Drawing Conclusions About ❏ Unit Six Resource Book: Active Reading SkillBuilder, p. 13
      Author's Purposes

Teaching the Literature
____ Reading the Selection

❏ PE pp. 950–958
❏ Unit Six Resource Book: Summary, p. 12

Thinking Through the Literature
____ Connect to the Literature
____ Think Critically ❏ Reading and Critical Thinking Transparencies, T4, T19
____ Extend Interpretations
____ Literary Analysis: Autobiographical Essay ❏ Literary Analysis Transparencies, T20

Choices and Challenges
Writing Options
____ Proposal for School Assembly
____ Autobiographical Essay

Vocabulary in Action
____ Meaning Clues

____ **Author Activity**

Copyright © McDougal Littell Inc.

How It Feels to Be Colored Me

Teaching Options (from Teacher's Edition)

Mini Lessons

Preteaching Vocabulary
____ Using Context Clues

Vocabulary Strategy
____ Using Context Clues with Figurative Language   ❏ Vocabulary Transparencies and Copymasters, C79

Grammar
____ Modifiers: Distinguishing *Those* from *Them*   ❏ Grammar Transparencies and Copymasters, C138

Viewing and Representing
Art Appreciation
____ *Skipping Along* by Stephen Scott Young
____ *Bal Jeunesse* by Palmer Hayden

Informal Assessment
____ Writing Letters to the Author

Assessment
____ Selection Quiz   ❏ Unit Six Resource Book: Selection Quiz, p. 16
____ Selection Test   ❏ Formal Assessment: Selection Test, pp. 175–176
____ Test Generator

Homework Assignments
_____
_____
_____
_____
_____

Other Teaching Materials
_____
_____
_____
_____

Copyright © McDougal Littell Inc.

My Dungeon Shook

Core Objectives
- Understand and appreciate an open letter
- Analyze characteristics of clearly written texts

Integrating Skills

Grammar
- Parallel Compound Predicates

Vocabulary
- Using Context to Determine Connotations
- Denotation and Connotation

Preparing to Read

____ Comparing Literature
____ Build Background
____ Vocabulary Preview: Using Context to Determine Connotations   ❑ Unit Six Resource Book: Words to Know SkillBuilder, p. 20
____ Focus Your Reading
     Literary Analysis: Open Letter   ❑ Unit Six Resource Book: Literary Analysis SkillBuilder, p. 19
     Active Reading: Analyzing Characteristics of   ❑ Unit Six Resource Book: Active Reading SkillBuilder, p. 18
     Clearly Written Texts

Teaching the Literature

____ Reading the Selection   ❑ PE pp. 959–966
     ❑ Unit One Resource Book: Summary, p.17

Thinking Through the Literature

____ Connect to the Literature
____ Think Critically   ❑ Reading and Critical Thinking Transparencies, T15
____ Extend Interpretations
____ Literary Analysis: Open Letter   ❑ Literary Analysis Transparencies, T23

Choices and Challenges

Writing Options
____ Points of Comparison
____ Personal Response
____ Compare-Contrast Essay

Activities and Explorations
____ Commencement Address
____ Photo Gallery of Harlem
____ Group Discussion

Inquiry and Research
____ Music

Vocabulary in Action
____ Context Clues

Copyright © McDougal Littell Inc.

My Dungeon Shook

Teaching Options (from Teacher's Edition)

Mini Lessons

Preteaching Vocabulary
____ Using Context to Determine Connotation

Vocabulary Strategy
____ Denotation and Connotation ❏ Vocabulary Transparencies and Copymasters, C80

Grammar
____ Parallel Compound Predicates ❏ Grammar Transparencies and Copymasters, C165, T57

Viewing and Representing
Art Appreciation
____ *My Brother* by John Wilson

Informal Assessment
____ Making Inferences and Generalizations

Assessment
____ Selection Quiz ❏ Unit Six Resource Book: Selection Quiz, p. 21
____ Selection Test ❏ Formal Assessment: Selection Test, pp. 177–178
____ Test Generator

Homework Assignments

_____

_____

_____

_____

Other Teaching Materials

_____

_____

_____

_____

Copyright © McDougal Littell Inc.

Life for My Child Is Simple / Primer for Blacks   Pages 967–972

Core Objectives
- Understand and appreciate two poems
- Identify and examine style in poetry
- Compare and contrast poems

Integrating Skills

Grammar
- Parallel Series

Vocabulary
- Prefixes

Preparing to Read
____ Comparing Literature
____ Build Background
____ Focus Your Reading
     Literary Analysis: Style   ❑ Unit Six Resource Book: Literary Analysis SkillBuilder, p. 23
     Active Reading: Comparing and Contrasting   ❑ Unit Six Resource Book: Active Reading SkillBuilder, p. 22
       Poems

Teaching the Literature
____ Reading the Selection   ❑ PE pp. 967–972

Thinking Through the Literature
____ Connect to the Literature
____ Think Critically   ❑ Reading and Critical Thinking Transparencies, T15, T41
____ Extend Interpretations
____ Literary Analysis: Style

Choices and Challenges
Writing Options
____ Points of Comparison
____ Yearbook Biography
____ Summary of Brooks's Message

Activities and Explorations
____ T-shirt Emblem
____ Preach a Sermon

____ **Author Activity**

Copyright © McDougal Littell Inc.

Life for My Child Is Simple / Primer for Blacks

Teaching Options (from Teacher's Edition)

Mini Lessons

Vocabulary Strategy

____ Prefixes

❑ Vocabulary Transparencies and Copymasters, C81

Grammar

____ Parallel Series

❑ Grammar Transparencies and Copymasters, C166, T54, T57

Speaking and Listening

____ Roundtable Discussion

Informal Assessment

____ Predicting Probable Outcomes

Assessment

____ Selection Test

____ Test Generator

❑ Formal Assessment: Selection Test, pp. 179–180

Homework Assignments

_____

_____

_____

_____

_____

Other Teaching Materials

_____

_____

_____

_____

Copyright © McDougal Littell Inc.

Thoughts on the African-American Novel

Core Objectives
- Understand and appreciate an essay of literary criticism
- Identify major ideas in an essay

Integrating Skills

Grammar
- Varying Sentence Beginnings

Vocabulary
- Greek and Latin Roots

Preparing to Read

____ Comparing Literature

____ Build Background

____ Focus Your Reading

Literary Analysis: Literary Criticism   ❏ Unit Six Resource Book: Literary Analysis SkillBuilder, p. 26

Active Reading: Identifying Major Ideas   ❏ Unit Six Resource Book: Active Reading SkillBuilder, p. 25

Teaching the Literature

____ Reading the Selection

❏ PE pp. 973–977
❏ Unit Six Resource Book: Summary, p. 24

Thinking Through the Literature

____ Connect to the Literature

____ Think Critically   ❏ Reading and Critical Thinking Transparencies, T12, T51, T60

____ Extend Interpretations

____ Literary Analysis: Literary Criticism

Choices and Challenges

Writing Options

____ Letter to Toni Morrison

____ Points of Comparison

____ Essay About Art Form

Activities and Explorations

____ Illustration

Inquiry and Research

____ Origin of the Novel

Author Activity

Copyright © McDougal Littell Inc.

Thoughts on the African-American Novel

Teaching Options (from Teacher's Edition)

Mini Lessons

Vocabulary Strategy

____ Greek and Latin Roots ❑ Vocabulary Transparencies and Copymasters, C82

Grammar

____ Varying Sentence Beginnings ❑ Grammar Transparencies and Copymasters, C167

Informal Assessment

____ Using a Chorus

Assessment

____ Selection Quiz ❑ Unit Six Resource Book: Selection Quiz, p. 27

____ Selection Test ❑ Formal Assessment: Selection Test, p. 181

____ Part Test ❑ Formal Assessment: Unit Six, Part 1 Test, pp. 183–184

____ Test Generator

Homework Assignments

_____

_____

_____

_____

_____

Other Teaching Materials

_____

_____

_____

_____

Copyright © McDougal Littell Inc.

Research Report

Writing Prompt
Write a historical research report about some aspect
of the Harlem Renaissance or another topic that
your teacher approves.

Preparing

___ Introduction

___ Basics in a Box

___ Using the Graphic

___ Analyzing a Student Model
"Zora Neale Hurston"

❑ Writing Transparencies and Copymasters, T11, T20, C33

❑ Unit Six Resource Book: Student Models, pp. 34–39

Writing

___ **Prewriting and Exploring**
Choosing a Subject
Planning the Research Report
Researching

___ **Drafting**
Organizing the Draft

___ **Peer Review**
Ask Your Peer Reader

___ **Revising**
Elaborating—Details and Examples

___ **Editing and Proofreading**
Using Commas

___ **Reflecting**

❑ Unit Six Resource Book: Prewriting, p. 29

❑ Unit Six Resource Book: Drafting and Elaboration, p. 30

❑ Unit Six Resource Book: Peer Response Guide, pp. 31–32

❑ Unit Six Resource Book: Revising, Editing, and Proofreading, p. 33
❑ Unit Six Resource Book: Rubric for Evaluation, p. 40

Homework Assignments

_____

_____

_____

_____

_____

Other Teaching Materials

_____

_____

_____

_____

_____

Copyright © McDougal Littell Inc.

Selected Poems by Robert Frost

Core Objectives
- Understand and appreciate classic poetry
- Identify and examine mood in poetry
- Analyze word choice

Integrating Skills
Grammar
- Adjective Elements

Vocabulary
- Connotation and Denotation

Preparing to Read
____ Connect to Your Life
____ Build Background
____ Focus Your Reading

Literary Analysis: Mood in Poetry   ❑ Unit Six Resource Book: Literary Analysis SkillBuilder, p. 44

Active Reading: Analyzing Word Choice   ❑ Unit Six Resource Book: Active Reading SkillBuilder, p. 43

Teaching the Literature
____ Reading the Selection   ❑ PE pp. 1000–1005

Thinking Through the Literature
____ Connect to the Literature
____ Think Critically   ❑ Reading and Critical Thinking Transparencies, T50
____ Extend Interpretations
____ Literary Analysis: Mood   ❑ Literary Analysis Transparencies, T18

Teaching Options (from Teacher's Edition)

Mini Lessons

Vocabulary Strategy
____ Discriminate Between Connotation and   ❑ Vocabulary Transparencies and Copymasters, C83
        Denotation

Grammar
____ Adjective Elements   ❑ Grammar Transparencies and Copymasters, C141

Cross Curricular Link

History
____ The Berlin Wall

Informal Assessment
____ Make Inferences and Draw Conclusions

Copyright © McDougal Littell Inc.

Selected Poems by Robert Frost

Assessment

____ Selection Test

____ Test Generator

❑ Formal Assessment: Selection Test, pp. 185–186

Homework Assignments

_____

_____

_____

_____

_____

Other Teaching Materials

_____

_____

_____

_____

_____

Copyright © McDougal Littell Inc.

Name _____ *Date* _____

The Death of the Hired Man

Pages 1006–1015

Core Objectives
- Understand and appreciate a narrative poem
- Examine blank verse
- Understand form in poetry

Integrating Skills

Grammar
- Modifiers

Vocabulary
- Using Context Clues
- Connotation

Preparing to Read
____ Connect to Your Life
____ Build Background
____ Vocabulary Preview: Using Context Clues: ❏ Unit Six Resource Book: Words to Know SkillBuilder, p. 48
Summary Statements
____ Focus Your Reading
Literary Analysis: Blank Verse   ❏ Unit Six Resource Book: Literary Analysis SkillBuilder, p. 47
Active Reading: Understanding Form in Poetry   ❏ Unit Six Resource Book: Active Reading SkillBuilder, p. 46

Teaching the Literature
❏ PE pp. 1006–1015
____ Reading the Selection   ❏ Unit Six Resource Book: Summary, p. 45

Thinking Through the Literature
____ Connect to the Literature
____ Think Critically   ❏ Reading and Critical Thinking Transparencies, T26
____ Extend Interpretations
____ Literary Analysis: Blank Verse   ❏ Literary Analysis Transparencies, T12

Choices and Challenges

Writing Options
____ Neighborly Editorial

Activities and Explorations
____ New England Collage

Inquiry and Research
____ Farm Life

Vocabulary in Action
____ Synonyms

Author Study Presentation
____ Living Museum Project

Copyright © McDougal Littell Inc.

Teaching Options (from Teacher's Edition)

Mini Lessons

Preteaching Vocabulary

____ Using Context Clues: Summary Statements

Vocabulary Strategy

____ Interpret the Connotative Power of Words   ❑ Vocabulary Transparencies and Copymasters, C84

Grammar

____ Problems with Modifiers: *This, These, That, Those*   ❑ Grammar Transparencies and Copymasters, C139

Cross Curricular Link

Workplace

____ Communicating Ideas

Informal Assessment

____ Journal Entries

Assessment

____ Selection Quiz   ❑ Unit Six Resource Book: Selection Quiz, p. 49

____ Selection Test   ❑ Formal Assessment: Selection Test, pp. 187–188

____ Test Generator

Homework Assignments

_____

_____

_____

_____

_____

Other Teaching Materials

_____

_____

_____

_____

_____

Copyright © McDougal Littell Inc.

Core Objectives
- Understand a modernist short story
- Identify and examine style
- Make inferences in a short story

Integrating Skills

Grammar
- Modifiers: Illogical Comparisons
- Commas with Direct Quotations

Vocabulary
- Relying on Context to Determine Connotation

Preparing to Read
____ Connect to Your Life
____ Build Background
____ Focus Your Reading
    Literary Analysis: Style   ❑ Unit Six Resource Book: Literary Analysis SkillBuilder, p. 52
    Active Reading: Making Inferences   ❑ Unit Six Resource Book: Active Reading SkillBuilder, p. 51

Teaching the Literature
____ Reading the Selection   ❑ PE pp. 1018–1024
    ❑ Unit Six Resource Book: Summary, p. 50

Thinking Through the Literature
____ Connect to the Literature
____ Think Critically   ❑ Reading and Critical Thinking Transparencies, T7
____ Extend Interpretations
____ Literary Analysis: Style   ❑ Literary Analysis Transparencies, T17

Choices and Challenges

Writing Options
____ Personal Ad
____ Advice Letters
____ TV Script

Activities and Explorations
____ Story Illustrations
____ Survey of Romantic Breakups

Copyright © McDougal Littell Inc.

Teaching Options (from Teacher's Edition)

Mini Lessons

Vocabulary Strategy
____ Relying on Context to Determine
Connotations of Words

❑ Vocabulary Transparencies and Copymasters, C85

Grammar
____ Modifiers: Illogical Comparisons
____ Commas: Setting Off Quotations

❑ Grammar Transparencies and Copymasters, C134
❑ Grammar Transparencies and Copymasters, C154, T56

Viewing and Representing
Art Appreciation
____ *Canoe* by David Park

Informal Assessment
____ Story Map

Assessment
____ Selection Quiz
____ Selection Test
____ Test Generator

❑ Unit Six Resource Book: Selection Quiz, p. 53
❑ Formal Assessment: Selection Test, pp. 189–190

Homework Assignments

_____

_____

_____

_____

Other Teaching Materials

_____

_____

_____

_____

Copyright © McDougal Littell Inc.

The Love Song of J. Alfred Prufrock

Core Objectives
- Understand and appreciate a classic modernist poem
- Identify and appreciate imagery
- Understand stream of consciousness

Integrating Skills

Grammar
- Inverted Subjects and Verbs

Vocabulary
- Context Clues
- Understanding Figurative Language Through Context

Preparing to Read
____ Connect to Your Life
____ Build Background
____ Vocabulary Preview: Context Clues   ❏ Unit Six Resource Book: Words to Know SkillBuilder, p. 57
____ Focus Your Reading
       Literary Analysis: Imagery   ❏ Unit Six Resource Book: Literary Analysis SkillBuilder, p. 56
       Active Reading: Understanding Stream of ❏ Unit Six Resource Book: Active Reading SkillBuilder, p. 55
       Consciousness

Teaching the Literature
____ Reading the Selection   ❏ PE pp. 1025–1032
                                              ❏ Unit Six Resource Book: Summary, p. 54

Thinking Through the Literature
____ Connect to the Literature
____ Think Critically   ❏ Reading and Critical Thinking Transparencies, T9
____ Extend Interpretations
____ Literary Analysis: Imagery   ❏ Literary Analysis Transparencies, T17

Choices and Challenges

Writing Options
____ Letter to Prufrock
____ Partygoers Narrative
____ Social Commentary

Activities and Explorations
____ Improvisational Scene
____ Prufrock's Caricature
____ Radio Talk Show

Inquiry and Research
____ Michelangelo's Artistic Genius

Vocabulary in Action
____ Synonyms
____ Exercise B

Copyright © McDougal Littell Inc.

The Love Song of J. Alfred Prufrock

Choices and Challenges (continued)

Author Activity

____ Broadway Smash Hit

Teaching Options (from Teacher's Edition)

Mini Lessons

Preteaching Vocabulary

____ Context Clues

❏ Vocabulary Transparencies and Copymasters, C86

Vocabulary Strategy

____ Understanding Figurative Language Through Context

Grammar

____ Inverted Subjects and Verbs

❏ Grammar Transparencies and Copymasters, C78

Cross Curricular Link

Humanities

____ Modernism

Informal Assessment

____ Making Inferences and Drawing Conclusions

Assessment

____ Selection Quiz

____ Selection Test

____ Test Generator

❏ Unit Six Resource Book: Selection Quiz, p. 58

❏ Formal Assessment: Selection Test, pp. 191–192

Homework Assignments

_____

_____

_____

_____

Other Teaching Materials

_____

_____

_____

_____

Copyright © McDougal Littell Inc.

The Jilting of Granny Weatherall

Core Objectives
- Understand and appreciate a modernist short story
- Understand a stream-of-consciousness narrative
- Use sequencing to untangle events

Integrating Skills

Grammar
- Parallel Compound Subjects
- Colon

Vocabulary
- Using Context Clues
- Figurative Language and Idioms

Preparing to Read
____ Connect to Your Life
____ Build Background
____ Vocabulary Preview: Context Clues   ❏ Unit Six Resource Book: Words to Know SkillBuilder, p. 62
____ Focus Your Reading
        Literary Analysis: Stream of Consciousness   ❏ Unit Six Resource Book: Literary Analysis SkillBuilder, p. 61
        Active Reading: Sequencing   ❏ Unit Six Resource Book: Active Reading SkillBuilder, p. 60

Teaching the Literature
                                                         ❏ PE pp. 1034–1044
____ Reading the Selection   ❏ Unit Six Resource Book: Summary, p. 59

Thinking Through the Literature
____ Connect to the Literature
____ Think Critically
____ Extend Interpretations
____ Literary Analysis: Stream of Consciousness   ❏ Literary Analysis Transparencies, T17

Choices and Challenges

Writing Options
____ Eulogy for Granny
____ Psychological Profile

Activities and Explorations
____ Story Illustration
____ Tabloid Interview

Vocabulary in Action
____ Analogies

Copyright © McDougal Littell Inc.

The Jilting of Granny Weatherall

Teaching Options (from Teacher's Edition)

Mini Lessons

Preteaching Vocabulary
____ Context Clues

Vocabulary Strategy
____ Using Context Clues for Figurative
Language and Idioms

❑ Vocabulary Transparencies and Copymasters, C87

Grammar
____ Parallel Compound Subjects
____ Colon as a Sentence Connector

❑ Grammar Transparencies and Copymasters, C168
❑ Grammar Transparencies and Copymasters, C159, T57

Viewing and Representing
Art Appreciation
____ *Portrait of Ambroise Vollard* by Pablo Picasso
____ *Yvonne and Magdaleine Torn in Tatters*
by Marcel Duchamp

Cross Curricular Link

Women's Studies
____ Role of Antebellum Southern Women

Informal Assessment
____ Understanding Character

Assessment

____ Selection Quiz
____ Selection Test
____ Test Generator

❑ Unit Six Resource Book: Selection Quiz, p. 63
❑ Formal Assessment: Selection Test, pp. 193–194

Homework Assignments

_____

_____

_____

_____

_____

Other Teaching Materials

_____

_____

_____

_____

_____

Copyright © McDougal Littell Inc.

The Man Who Was Almost a Man

Core Objectives
- Understand and appreciate a short story
- Understand point of view
- Make judgments about the main character's decisions

Integrating Skills

Grammar
- Creating Complex Sentences
- Quotation Marks with Other Punctuation

Vocabulary
- Dictionaries and Slang

Preparing to Read
____ Connect to Your Life
____ Build Background
____ Focus Your Reading
    Literary Analysis: Point of View
    Active Reading: Making Judgments

❑ Unit Six Resource Book: Literary Analysis SkillBuilder, p. 66
❑ Unit Six Resource Book: Active Reading SkillBuilder, p. 65

Teaching the Literature
____ Reading the Selection

❑ PE pp. 1045–1056
❑ Unit Six Resource Book: Summary, p. 64

Thinking Through the Literature
____ Connect to the Literature
____ Think Critically
____ Extend Interpretations
____ Literary Analysis: Point of View

❑ Reading and Critical Thinking Transparencies, T5

❑ Literary Analysis Transparencies, T20

Choices and Challenges

Writing Options
____ Defining Adulthood
____ Letter Home
____ Editorial

Activities and Explorations
____ Dramatic Reading
____ Charting Expenses
____ Film Critics' Circle

Author Activity
____ The Creation of Characters

Copyright © McDougal Littell Inc.

The Man Who Was Almost a Man

Teaching Options (from Teacher's Edition)

Mini Lessons

Vocabulary Strategy

____ Dictionaries and Slang

❏ Vocabulary Transparencies and Copymasters, C88

Grammar

____ Creating Complex Sentences

____ Quotation Marks with Other Punctuation

❏ Grammar Transparencies and Copymasters, C169

❏ Grammar Transparencies and Copymasters, C162, T56

Speaking and Listening

____ Pronunciation of Dialect

Viewing and Representing

____ Photographs

Cross Curricular Links

U.S. History

____ 1910

Economics

____ African-American Sharecroppers in the Early 20th Century

Workplace

____ Writing an Evaluation

Informal Assessment

____ Predicting What Happens Next

Assessment

____ Selection Quiz

____ Selection Test

____ Test Generator

❏ Unit Six Resource Book: Selection Quiz, p. 67

❏ Formal Assessment: Selection Test, pp. 195–196

Homework Assignments

_____

_____

_____

_____

_____

Other Teaching Materials

_____

_____

_____

_____

_____

Copyright © McDougal Littell Inc.

Mirror / Self in 1958

Core Objectives
- Understand and appreciate two confessional poems
- Identify and examine the speaker in poetry
- Link title and theme

Integrating Skills

Grammar
- Compound Sentences
- Capitalizing Family Titles

Vocabulary
- Word Origins: Mirror

Preparing to Read
____ Comparing Literature
____ Build Background
____ Focus Your Reading
    Literary Analysis: Speaker   ❑ Unit Six Resource Book: Literary Analysis SkillBuilder, p. 69
    Active Reading: Linking Title and Theme   ❑ Unit Six Resource Book: Active Reading SkillBuilder, p. 68

Teaching the Literature
____ Reading the Selection   ❑ PE pp. 1057–1063

Thinking Through the Literature
____ Connect to the Literature
____ Think Critically   ❑ Reading and Critical Thinking Transparencies, T48
____ Extend Interpretations
____ Literary Analysis: Speaker   ❑ Literary Analysis Transparencies, T23

Choices and Challenges

Writing Options
____ Diary of a Housewife
____ Poetic Riddle
____ Points of Comparison

Activities and Explorations
____ Face-to-Face Conversation
____ A Doll's House

Inquiry and Research
____ Women's Roles
____ Confessional Poets

Copyright © McDougal Littell Inc.

Teaching Options (from Teacher's Edition)

Mini Lessons

Vocabulary Strategy
____ Researching Word Origins: Mirror   ❏ Vocabulary Transparencies and Copymasters, C89

Grammar
____ Creating Compound Sentences   ❏ Grammar Transparencies and Copymasters, C170
____ Capitalizing Family Titles   ❏ Grammar Transparencies and Copymasters, C143

Informal Assessment
____ Making Inferences

Assessment
____ Selection Test   ❏ Formal Assessment: Selection Test, pp. 197–198
____ Part Test   ❏ Formal Assessment: Unit Six, Part 2, pp. 199–200
____ Test Generator

Homework Assignments

_____
_____
_____
_____
_____

Other Teaching Materials

_____
_____
_____
_____

Copyright © McDougal Littell Inc.

Armistice

Core Objectives
- Understand and appreciate a short story
- Explore connections between theme and title
- Draw conclusions about character motivation

Integrating Skills

Grammar
- Complements

Vocabulary
- Using Context Clues
- Applying Meanings of Prefixes

Preparing to Read
____ Connect to Your Life
____ Build Background
____ Vocabulary Preview: Using Context Clues   ❏ Unit Seven Resource Book: Words to Know SkillBuilder, p. 7
____ Focus Your Reading
      Literary Analysis: Theme and Title   ❏ Unit Seven Resource Book: Literary Analysis SkillBuilder, p. 6
      Active Reading: Drawing Conclusions About   ❏ Unit Seven Resource Book: Active Reading SkillBuilder, p. 5
       Character Motivation

Teaching the Literature
❏ PE pp. 1076–1087
____ Reading the Selection   ❏ Unit Seven Resource Book: Summary, p. 4

Thinking Through the Literature
____ Connect to the Literature
____ Think Critically   ❏ Reading and Critical Thinking Transparencies, T4
____ Extend Interpretations
____ Literary Analysis: Theme and Title   ❏ Literary Analysis Transparencies, T20

Choices and Challenges

Writing Options
____ Dream Analysis
____ Letter to the Editor
____ Eventful Paragraph
____ World War II Presentation

Activities and Explorations
____ Readers Theater Performance
____ Memory Illustration

Inquiry and Research
____ History of Anti-Semitism
____ German Victory

Art Connection
____ Conflicting Impression

Copyright © McDougal Littell Inc.

Armistice

Choices and Challenges (continued)

Vocabulary in Action
____ Context Clues

Author Activity
____ Grave Pronouncement

Teaching Options (from Teacher's Edition)

Mini Lessons

Preteaching Vocabulary
____ Using Context Clues

Vocabulary Strategy
____ Applying Meanings of Prefixes   ❏ Vocabulary Transparencies and Copymasters, C90

Grammar
____ Complements   ❏ Grammar Transparencies and Copymasters, C79

Speaking and Listening
____ Role Playing

Viewing and Representing
Art Appreciation
____ *What Will Become of Us?* by George Skirigin
____ Photograph

Cross Curricular Link

History
____ Summary of Major Events of World War II

Informal Assessment
____ Understanding Character and Style

Assessment
____ Selection Quiz   ❏ Unit Seven Resource Book: Selection Quiz, p. 8
____ Selection Test   ❏ Formal Assessment: Selection Test, pp. 201–202
____ Test Generator

Homework Assignments

_____

_____

_____

_____

_____

Other Teaching Materials

_____

_____

_____

_____

_____

Copyright © McDougal Littell Inc.

The Death of the Ball Turret Gunner / Why Soldiers Won't Talk

Core Objectives
- Understand and appreciate a poem and an essay
- Understand how imagery conveys tone
- Adjust reading strategies for different genres

Integrating Skills

Grammar	Vocabulary
- Rhythm vs. Redundancy	- Suffixes

Preparing to Read
____ Connect to Your Life
____ Build Background
____ Focus Your Reading:
     Literary Analysis: Imagery and Tone   ❑ Unit Seven Resource Book: Literary Analysis SkillBuilder, p. 11
     Active Reading: Adjusting Reading Strategies   ❑ Unit Seven Resource Book: Active Reading SkillBuilder, p. 10

Teaching the Literature
     ❑ PE pp. 1088–1094
____ Reading the Selection   ❑ Unit Seven Resource Book: Summary, p. 9

Thinking Through the Literature
____ Connect to the Literature
____ Think Critically   ❑ Reading and Critical Thinking Transparencies, T8, T12, T39
____ Extend Interpretations
____ Literary Analysis: Imagery and Tone

Choices and Challenges
Writing Options
____ Grave Inscriptions
____ Personal Narrative

Activities and Explorations
____ Interview with a Veteran
____ Model Plane

Inquiry and Research
____ Shell Shock

Copyright © McDougal Littell Inc.

The Death of the Ball Turret Gunner /
Why Soldiers Won't Talk

Teaching Options (from Teacher's Edition)

Mini Lessons

Vocabulary Strategy

____ Suffixes

❑ Vocabulary Transparencies and Copymasters, C91

Grammar

____ Rhythm: Repetition vs. Redundancy

❑ Grammar Transparencies and Copymasters, C171

Speaking and Listening

____ Interview

Informal Assessment

____ Write a Letter

Assessment

____ Selection Quiz

❑ Unit Seven Resource Book: Selection Quiz, p. 12

____ Selection Test

❑ Formal Assessment: Selection Test, pp. 203–204

____ Test Generator

Homework Assignments

_____

_____

_____

_____

_____

Other Teaching Materials

_____

_____

_____

_____

_____

Copyright © McDougal Littell Inc.

Letter from Paradise /
In Response to Executive Order 9066

Core Objectives
- Understand and appreciate an essay and a poem
- Understand mood
- Compare mood in an essay and a poem

Integrating Skills

Grammar
- The Placement of *Only*

Vocabulary
- Prefixes

Preparing to Read
____ Connect to Your Life
____ Build Background
____ Focus Your Reading
    Literary Analysis: Mood   ❑ Unit Seven Resource Book: Literary Analysis SkillBuilder, p. 15
    Active Reading: Comparing Mood   ❑ Unit Seven Resource Book: Active Reading SkillBuilder, p. 14

Teaching the Literature
                                        ❑ PE pp. 1095–1102
____ Reading the Selection   ❑ Unit Seven Resource Book: Summary, p. 13

Thinking Through the Literature
____ Connect to the Literature
____ Think Critically   ❑ Reading and Critical Thinking Transparencies, T15
____ Extend Interpretations
____ Literary Analysis: Mood   ❑ Literary Analysis Transparencies, T20

Choices and Challenges
Writing Options
____ Family Memoir

Activities and Explorations
____ Contrasting Cartoons

Inquiry and Research
____ Japanese-American Internment

Copyright © McDougal Littell Inc.

Letter from Paradise /
In Response to Executive Order 9066

Teaching Options (from Teacher's Edition)

Mini Lessons

Vocabulary Strategy
___ Prefixes

❏ Vocabulary Transparencies and Copymasters, C90

Grammar
___ The Placement of *Only*

Speaking and Listening
___ Poem Recitation

Cross Curricular Link

History
___ Pearl Harbor

Informal Assessment

___ Understanding Mood

Assessment
___ Selection Quiz
___ Selection Test
___ Test Generator

❏ Unit Seven Resource Book: Selection Quiz, p. 16
❏ Formal Assessment: Selection Test, pp. 205–206

Homework Assignments

_____
_____
_____
_____
_____

Other Teaching Materials

_____
_____
_____
_____
_____

Copyright © McDougal Littell Inc.

Ambush

Core Objectives
- Understand and appreciate a short story
- Understand internal conflict
- Connect the story to personal experience

Integrating Skills

Grammar	Vocabulary
■ Adverbs: Qualifiers	■ Context Clues

Preparing to Read
___ Comparing Literature
___ Build Background
___ Focus Your Reading:
    Literary Analysis: Internal Conflict   ❑ Unit Seven Resource Book: Literary Analysis SkillBuilder, p. 19
    Active Reading: Connecting to Experience   ❑ Unit Seven Resource Book: Active Reading SkillBuilder, p. 18

Teaching the Literature
                                   ❑ PE pp. 1105–1110
___ Reading the Selection   ❑ Unit Seven Resource Book: Summary, p. 17

Thinking Through the Literature
___ Connect to the Literature
___ Think Critically   ❑ Reading and Critical Thinking Transparencies, T9, T58
___ Extend Interpretations
___ Literary Analysis: Internal Conflict   ❑ Literary Analysis Transparencies, T15

Choices and Challenges

Writing Options
___ Exhibit Proposal
___ Points of Comparison

Activities and Explorations
___ Movie Score

Inquiry and Research
___ Guerrilla Tactics

Author Activity
___ Real-Life Experience

Copyright © McDougal Littell Inc.

Teaching Options (from Teacher's Edition)

Mini Lessons

Vocabulary Strategy

____ Context Clues

❏ Vocabulary Transparencies and Copymasters, C92

Grammar

____ Adverbs: Qualifiers

❏ Grammar Transparencies and Copymasters, C71

Viewing and Representing

Art Appreciation

____ *Fenixes* by Rupert Garcia

Assessment

____ Selection Quiz

____ Selection Test

____ Test Generator

❏ Unit Seven Resource Book: Selection Quiz, p. 20

❏ Formal Assessment: Selection Test, pp. 207–208

Homework Assignments

_____

_____

_____

_____

_____

Other Teaching Materials

_____

_____

_____

_____

Copyright © McDougal Littell Inc.

Camouflaging the Chimera / Deciding

Core Objectives
- Understand and appreciate two poems about the Vietnam War
- Understand the speaker in poetry
- Examine structure in poetry

Integrating Skills

Grammar
- Punctuation: Capitalization

Vocabulary
- Using Context to Understand Figurative Language

Preparing to Read
____ Comparing Literature
____ Build Background
____ Focus Your Reading
　　　Literary Analysis: Speaker in Poetry　　　❑ Unit Seven Resource Book: Literary Analysis SkillBuilder, p. 22
　　　Active Reading: Structure in Poetry　　　❑ Unit Seven Resource Book: Active Reading SkillBuilder, p. 21

Teaching the Literature
____ Reading the Selection　　　　　　　　❑ PE pp. 1111–1117

Thinking Through the Literature
____ Connect to the Literature
____ Think Critically　　　　　　　　　　　❑ Reading and Critical Thinking Transparencies, T15, T17
____ Extend Interpretations
____ Literary Analysis: Speaker in Poetry

Choices and Challenges
Writing Options
____ Points of Comparison

Inquiry and Research
____ Environmental Effects of War

Copyright © McDougal Littell Inc.

Teaching Options (from Teacher's Edition)

Mini Lessons

Vocabulary Strategy
____ Using Context to Understand Figurative Language

❏ Vocabulary Transparencies and Copymasters, C93

Grammar
____ Punctuation: Capitalization

❏ Grammar Transparencies and Copymasters, C145, C171

Informal Assessment
____ Letter Writing

Assessment
____ Selection Test
____ Test Generator

❏ Formal Assessment: Selection Test, pp. 209–210

Homework Assignments

_____
_____
_____
_____
_____

Other Teaching Materials

_____
_____
_____
_____
_____

Copyright © McDougal Littell Inc.

At the Justice Department, November 15, 1969

Pages 1118–1121

Core Objectives
- Understand and appreciate a protest poem
- Understand the elements of style
- Make inferences about meaning

Integrating Skills
Grammar
- Varying Sentence Closers

Preparing to Read
____ Comparing Literature
____ Build Background
____ Focus Your Reading
    Literary Analysis: Style   ❏ Unit Seven Resource Book: Literary Analysis SkillBuilder, p. 24
    Active Reading: Making Inferences   ❏ Unit Seven Resource Book: Active Reading SkillBuilder, p. 23
      About Meaning

Teaching the Literature
____ Reading the Selection   ❏ PE pp. 1118–1121

Thinking Through the Literature
____ Connect to the Literature
____ Think Critically   ❏ Reading and Critical Thinking Transparencies, T7, T52
____ Extend Interpretations
____ Literary Analysis: Style   ❏ Literary Analysis Transparencies, T23

Choices and Challenges
Writing Options
____ TV Script
____ Antiwar Storyboard
____ Points of Comparison

Activities and Explorations
____ Opinion Poster
____ War Debate

Inquiry and Research
____ Impact of Antiwar Protests

Copyright © McDougal Littell Inc.

At the Justice Department, November 15, 1969

Teaching Options (from Teacher's Edition)

Mini Lessons

Grammar

____ Varying Sentence Closers

❑ Grammar Transparencies and Copymasters, C172

Informal Assessment

____ Writing a Summary

Assessment

____ Selection Test

____ Part Test

____ Test Generator

❑ Formal Assessment: Selection Test, pp. 211–212

❑ Formal Assessment: Unit Seven, Part 1 Test, pp. 213–214

Homework Assignments

_____

_____

_____

_____

Other Teaching Materials

_____

_____

_____

Copyright © McDougal Littell Inc.

Multimedia Exhibit

Prompt
Create a multimedia exhibit about
a topic that interests you.

Preparing
____ Introduction
____ Basics in a Box
____ Presenting the Guidelines and Standards

____ Analyzing a Multimedia Exhibit
     "America at War"

Creating

____ **Planning the Multimedia Exhibit**   ❑ Unit Seven Resource Book: Planning Your Exhibit, p. 26

____ **Preparing the Exhibit**   ❑ Unit Seven Resource Book: Preparing Your Exhibit, p. 27

____ **Peer Review**   ❑ Unit Seven Resource Book: Peer Response Guide, pp. 28–29
     Ask Your Peer Reader

____ **Refining the Exhibit**   ❑ Unit Seven Resource Book: Refining Your Exhibit, p. 30
                                                  ❑ Unit Seven Resource Book: Standards for Evaluation, p. 31
____ **Reflecting**

Copyright © McDougal Littell Inc.

Homework Assignments	**Other Teaching Materials**
_____	_____
_____	_____
_____	_____
_____	_____

Letter from Birmingham Jail

Core Objectives
- Understand a historic letter
- Identify and examine allusion
- Understand logical argument: deduction and induction

Integrating Skills

Grammar
- Verbs: Voice and Mood

Vocabulary
- Using Context Clues
- Latin Roots

Preparing to Read
____ Connect to Your Life
____ Build Background
____ Vocabulary Preview: Using Context Clues   ❏ Unit Seven Resource Book: Words to Know SkillBuilder, p. 37
____ Focus Your Reading
     Literary Analysis: Allusion   ❏ Unit Seven Resource Book: Literary Analysis SkillBuilder, p. 36
     Active Reading: Logical Argument: Induction   ❏ Unit Seven Resource Book: Active Reading SkillBuilder, p. 35
     and Deduction

Teaching the Literature
                        ❏ PE pp. 1136–1147
____ Reading the Selection   ❏ Unit Seven Resource Book: Summary, p. 34

Thinking Through the Literature
____ Connect to the Literature
____ Think Critically   ❏ Reading and Critical Thinking Transparencies, T21
____ Extend Interpretations
____ Literary Analysis: Allusion

Choices and Challenges

Writing Options
____ Defining a Hero
____ Editorial About King's Ideas
____ Compare-and-Contrast Essay

Activities and Explorations
____ Poster Design
____ Dramatic Skit
____ Multimedia Presentation

Inquiry and Research
____ Civil Rights Today

Vocabulary in Action
____ Meaning Clues
____ Synonyms

Copyright © McDougal Littell Inc.

Letter from Birmingham Jail

Teaching Options (from Teacher's Edition)

Mini Lessons

Preteaching Vocabulary
_____ Using Context Clues

Vocabulary Strategy
_____ Latin Roots

❏ Vocabulary Transparencies and Copymasters, C94

Grammar
_____ Verbs: Voice and Mood

❏ Grammar Transparencies and Copymasters, C119

Speaking and Listening
_____ Persuasive Speech

Viewing and Representing
Art Appreciation
_____ Photographs as Chronicles

Cross Curricular Link

History
_____ Civil Rights Movement

Informal Assessment
_____ Choosing the Best Summary

Assessment

_____ Selection Quiz
_____ Selection Test
_____ Test Generator

❏ Formal Assessment: Selection Quiz, p. 38
❏ Formal Assessment: Selection Test, pp. 215–216

Homework Assignments

_____
_____
_____
_____
_____

Other Teaching Materials

_____
_____
_____
_____
_____

Copyright © McDougal Littell Inc.

Wandering

Core Objectives
- Understand and appreciate a one-act drama
- Examine tone and dialogue
- Visualize stage directions

Integrating Skills

Grammar
- Prepositional Phrases

Vocabulary
- Using Context Clues

Preparing to Read
____ Connect to Your Life
____ Build Background
____ Vocabulary Preview: Using Context Clues   ❑ Unit Seven Resource Book: Words to Know SkillBuilder, p. 42
____ Focus Your Reading
     Literary Analysis: Tone and Dialogue   ❑ Unit Seven Resource Book: Literary Analysis SkillBuilder, p. 41
     Active Reading: Visualizing Stage Directions   ❑ Unit Seven Resource Book: Active Reading SkillBuilder, p. 40

Teaching the Literature
       ❑ PE pp. 1150–1156
____ Reading the Selection   ❑ Unit Seven Resource Book: Summary, p. 39

Thinking Through the Literature
____ Connect to the Literature
____ Think Critically   ❑ Reading and Critical Thinking Transparencies, T8
____ Extend Interpretations
____ Literary Analysis: Tone and Dialogue   ❑ Literary Analysis Transparencies, T19

Choices and Challenges

Writing Options
____ Drama Review
____ Play Outline

Inquiry and Research
____ Youth Counterculture

Vocabulary in Action
____ Context Clues

Copyright © McDougal Littell Inc.

Wandering

Teaching Options (from Teacher's Edition)

Mini Lessons

Preteaching Vocabulary
____ Using Context Clues

Grammar
____ Proliferating Prepositional Phrases   ❑ Grammar Transparencies and Copymasters, C173

Speaking and Listening
____ Drama Reenactment

Cross Curricular Link

History
____ A Time of Upheaval and Protest

Informal Assessment
____ Self-Assessment

Assessment
____ Selection Quiz   ❑ Unit Seven Resource Book: Selection Quiz, p. 43
____ Selection Test   ❑ Formal Assessment: Selection Test, pp. 217–218
____ Test Generator

Homework Assignments

_____

_____

_____

_____

Other Teaching Materials

_____

_____

_____

_____

Copyright © McDougal Littell Inc.

Name _____ Date _____

The Writer in the Family

Pages 1157–1167

Core Objectives
- Understand and appreciate a short story
- Understand plot development
- Draw conclusions about character

Integrating Skills

Grammar
- Unnecessary Commas
- Active vs. Passive Voice

Vocabulary
- Using Context Clues

Preparing to Read
____ Connect to Your Life
____ Build Background
____ Vocabulary Preview: Using Context Clues   ❑ Unit Seven Resource Book: Words to Know SkillBuilder, p. 47
____ Focus Your Reading
Literary Analysis: Plot Development   ❑ Unit Seven Resource Book: Literary Analysis SkillBuilder, p. 46
Active Reading: Drawing Conclusions About   ❑ Unit Seven Resource Book: Active Reading SkillBuilder, p. 45
    Characters

Teaching the Literature
❑ PE pp. 1157–1167
____ Reading the Selection   ❑ Unit Seven Resource Book: Summary, p. 44

Thinking Through the Literature
____ Connect to the Literature
____ Think Critically   ❑ Reading and Critical Thinking Transparencies, T4, T54
____ Extend Interpretations
____ Literary Analysis: Plot Development

Choices and Challenges

Writing Options
____ True Obituary
____ Definition of Success

Activities and Explorations
____ Mourning Rituals

Inquiry and Research
____ Mourning Rituals

Vocabulary in Action
____ Context Clues

Copyright © McDougal Littell Inc.

Teaching Options (from Teacher's Edition)

Mini Lessons

Preteaching Vocabulary
____ Using Context Clues

Grammar
____ Unnecessary Commas   ❏ Grammar Transparencies and Copymasters, C155
____ Voice: Active vs. Passive ❏ Grammar Transparencies and Copymasters, C68

Workplace Link
____ Writing a Business Letter

Informal Assessment
____ Retelling

Assessment
____ Selection Quiz   ❏ Unit Seven Resource Book: Selection Quiz, p. 48
____ Selection Test   ❏ Formal Assessment: Selection Test, pp. 219–220
____ Test Generator

Homework Assignments

_____

_____

_____

_____

_____

Other Teaching Materials

_____

_____

_____

_____

_____

Copyright © McDougal Littell Inc.

Teenage Wasteland

Core Objectives
- Understand and appreciate a short story
- Understand protagonist and antagonist
- Recognize important details

Integrating Skills
Grammar
- Verbs: Progressive and Emphatic Forms

Vocabulary
- Synonyms and Antonyms

Preparing to Read
____ Connect to Your Life
____ Build Background
____ Vocabulary Preview: Synonyms and Antonyms   ❑ Unit Seven Resource Book: Words to Know SkillBuilder, p. 52
____ Focus Your Reading
  Literary Analysis: Character: Protagonist and Antagonist   ❑ Unit Seven Resource Book: Literary Analysis SkillBuilder, p. 51
  Active Reading: Recognizing Important Details   ❑ Unit Seven Resource Book: Active Reading SkillBuilder, p. 50

Teaching the Literature
❑ PE pp. 1168–1179
____ Reading the Selection   ❑ Unit Seven Resource Book: Summary, p. 49

Thinking Through the Literature
____ Connect to the Literature
____ Think Critically   ❑ Reading and Critical Thinking Transparencies, T9
____ Extend Interpretations
____ Literary Analysis: Protagonist and Antagonist

Choices and Challenges
Writing Options
____ Rewritten Episodes
____ Persuasive Speech

Activities and Explorations
____ Dramatic Scene

Vocabulary in Action
____ Synonyms and Antonyms

Copyright © McDougal Littell Inc.

Teaching Options (from Teacher's Edition)

Mini Lessons

Preteaching Vocabulary

____ Synonyms and Antonyms

Grammar

____ Verbs: Progressive and Emphatic Forms   ❑ Grammar Transparencies and Copymasters, C118

Speaking and Listening

____ Role-Playing

Viewing and Representing

Art Appreciation

____ *Table with Fruit* by David Park

____ *Girl Looking at Landscape* by Richard Diebenkorn

Informal Assessment

____ Self-Assessment

Assessment

____ Selection Quiz   ❑ Unit Seven Resource Book: Selection Quiz, p. 53

____ Selection Test   ❑ Formal Assessment: Selection Test, pp. 221–222

____ Test Generator

Homework Assignments

_____

_____

_____

_____

_____

Other Teaching Materials

_____

_____

_____

_____

_____

Copyright © McDougal Littell Inc.

Core Objectives
- Understand and appreciate a short story
- Understand dramatic irony
- Make predictions

Integrating Skills

Grammar   **Vocabulary**
- Advanced Sentences: ■ Context Clues
  Sentence Openers
- Advanced Sentences:
  Periodic Sentences

Preparing to Read
____ Connect to Your Life
____ Build Background
____ Vocabulary Preview: Context Clues   ❑ Unit Seven Resource Book: Words to Know SkillBuilder, p. 57
____ Focus Your Reading
     Literary Analysis: Dramatic Irony   ❑ Unit Seven Resource Book: Literary Analysis SkillBuilder, p. 56
     Active Reading: Making Predictions   ❑ Unit Seven Resource Book: Active Reading SkillBuilder, p. 55

Teaching the Literature   ❑ PE pp. 1180–1193
____ Reading the Selection   ❑ Unit Seven Resource Book: Summary, p. 54

Thinking Through the Literature
____ Connect to the Literature
____ Think Critically   ❑ Reading and Critical Thinking Transparencies, T2
____ Extend Interpretations
____ Literary Analysis: Dramatic Irony

Choices and Challenges
Writing Options
____ Diary Entry
____ Character Analysis
____ Story Forecast

Activities and Explorations
____ Staging a Scene

Vocabulary in Action
____ Synonyms
____ Assessment Practice

Copyright © McDougal Littell Inc.

Teaching Options (from Teacher's Edition)

Mini Lessons

Preteaching Vocabulary
____ Using Context Clues

Speaking and Listening
____ Performing a Scene

Grammar
____ Advanced Sentences: Sentence Openers

____ Advanced Sentences: Periodic Sentences

❑ Grammar Transparencies and Copymasters, C174

❑ Grammar Transparencies and Copymasters, C175

Viewing and Representing
Art Appreciation
____ *Frank Wallace* and *Claire White* by Fairfield Porter

Cross Curricular Links

Social Studies
____ Divorce Law

Workplace
____ Preparing for Projects

Informal Assessment
____ Adapting Point of View
____ Making Predictions

Assessment
____ Selection Quiz
____ Selection Test
____ Test Generator

❑ Unit Seven Resource Book: Selection Quiz, p. 58
❑ Formal Assessment: Selection Test, pp. 223–224

Homework Assignments

_____
_____
_____
_____
_____

Other Teaching Materials

_____
_____
_____
_____
_____

Copyright © McDougal Littell Inc.

Name _____ Date _____

Mexicans Begin Jogging / Legal Alien

Core Objectives
- Understand and appreciate two contemporary poems
- Examine tone in poetry
- Compare writers' attitudes

Integrating Skills

Grammar
- Varying Types of Sentences

Vocabulary
- Connotation

Preparing to Read
___ Connect to Your Life
___ Build Background
___ Focus Your Reading
    Literary Analysis: Tone   ❑ Unit Seven Resource Book: Literary Analysis SkillBuilder, p. 60
    Active Reading: Comparing Writers' Attitudes   ❑ Unit Seven Resource Book: Active Reading SkillBuilder, p. 59

Teaching the Literature
___ Reading the Selection   ❑ PE pp. 1194–1199

Thinking Through the Literature
___ Connect to the Literature
___ Think Critically   ❑ Reading and Critical Thinking Transparencies, T23
___ Extend Interpretations
___ Literary Analysis: Tone

Choices and Challenges

Writing Options
___ Guest Editorial

Inquiry and Research
___ The Title "Legal Alien"

Art Connection
___ Photographs

Copyright © McDougal Littell Inc.

Mexicans Begin Jogging / Legal Alien

Teaching Options (from Teacher's Edition)

Mini Lessons

Vocabulary Strategy

____ Interpreting the Connotative Power of Words

❏ Vocabulary Transparencies and Copymasters, C95

Grammar

____ Varying Types of Sentences

❏ Grammar Transparencies and Copymasters, C176

Assessment

____ Selection Test

____ Test Generator

❏ Formal Assessment: Selection Test, pp. 225–226

Homework Assignments

_____

_____

_____

_____

_____

Other Teaching Materials

_____

_____

_____

_____

_____

Copyright © McDougal Littell Inc.

Hostage

Core Objectives
- Understand and appreciate a short story
- Understand character
- Make judgments about character

Integrating Skills

Grammar
- Interrupting Elements

Vocabulary
- Using Context Clues
- Synonyms and Antonyms

Preparing to Read
____ Comparing Literature
____ Vocabulary Preview: Using Context Clues   ❏ Unit Seven Resource Book: Words to Know SkillBuilder, p. 64
____ Focus Your Reading
    Literary Analysis: Character   ❏ Unit Seven Resource Book: Literary Analysis SkillBuilder, p. 63
    Active Reading: Making Judgments   ❏ Unit Seven Resource Book: Active Reading SkillBuilder, p. 62
       About Character

Teaching the Literature
❏ PE pp. 1200–1214
____ Reading the Selection   ❏ Unit Seven Resource Book: Summary, p. 61

Thinking Through the Literature
____ Connect to the Literature
____ Think Critically   ❏ Reading and Critical Thinking Transparencies, T5, T57, T36–38
____ Extend Interpretations
____ Literary Analysis: Character: Tragic Hero   ❏ Literary Analysis Transparencies, T6

Choices and Challenges

Writing Options
____ Character Sketch
____ Expository Essay
____ Literary Review
____ Points of Comparison

Activities and Explorations
____ Role-Play
____ Drawing
____ Debate

Inquiry and Research
____ Crime Statistics

Vocabulary in Action
____ Synonyms and Antonyms
____ Context Clues

____ Author Activity

Copyright © McDougal Littell Inc.

Teaching Options (from Teacher's Edition)

Mini Lessons

Preteaching Vocabulary
____ Using Context Clues

Vocabulary Strategy
____ Synonyms and Antonyms

❑ Vocabulary Transparencies and Copymasters, C96

Grammar
____ Interrupting Elements: Descriptions
That Split Subject and Verb

❑ Grammar Transparencies and Copymasters, C177

Speaking and Listening
____ Storytelling
____ Interviewing

Viewing and Representing
Art Appreciation

Informal Assessment

____ Understanding Character
____ Choosing the Best Theme

Assessment

____ Selection Quiz
____ Selection Test
____ Part Test
____ Test Generator

❑ Unit Seven Resource Book: Selection Quiz, p. 65
❑ Formal Assessment: Selection Test, pp. 227–228

Homework Assignments

_____
_____
_____
_____
_____

Other Teaching Materials

_____
_____
_____
_____
_____

Copyright © McDougal Littell Inc.

Mother Tongue

Core Objectives
- Understand and appreciate a personal essay
- Identify main ideas and supporting details

Integrating Skills

Grammar	Vocabulary
■ Cohesion	■ Using Context Clues

Preparing to Read

____ Comparing Literature

____ Build Background

____ Vocabulary Preview: Using Context Clues   ❑ Unit Seven Resource Book: Words to Know SkillBuilder, p. 69

____ Focus Your Reading

       Literary Analysis: Personal Essay   ❑ Unit Seven Resource Book: Literary Analysis SkillBuilder, p. 68

       Active Reading: Identifying Main Ideas and   ❑ Unit Seven Resource Book: Active Reading SkillBuilder, p. 67
           Supporting Details

Teaching the Literature

                                           ❑ PE pp. 1215–1222

____ Reading the Selection   ❑ Unit Seven Resource Book: Summary, p. 66

Thinking Through the Literature

____ Connect to the Literature

____ Think Critically   ❑ Reading and Critical Thinking Transparencies, T47, T55

____ Extend Interpretations

____ Literary Analysis: Personal Essay

Choices and Challenges

Writing Options

____ Story Evaluation

____ Points of Comparison

Vocabulary in Action

____ Context Clues

Author Activity

____ Tan's Short Stories

Copyright © McDougal Littell Inc.

Mother Tongue

Teaching Options (from Teacher's Edition)

Mini Lessons

Preteaching Vocabulary
_____ Using Context Clues

Grammar
_____ Cohesion: Reader Expectation ❑ Grammar Transparencies and Copymasters, C178

Speaking and Listening
_____ Effective Listening Skills: Role-Play

Informal Assessment
_____ Letter of Complaint

Assessment
_____ Selection Quiz
_____ Selection Test
_____ Test Generator

❑ Unit Seven Resource Book: Selection Quiz, p. 70
❑ Formal Assessment: Selection Test, pp. 229–230

Homework Assignments	Other Teaching Materials

Copyright © McDougal Littell Inc.

The Latin Deli: An Ars Poetica

Core Objectives
- Understand and appreciate a poem about bicultural experience
- Understand and appreciate imagery
- Analyze descriptive details

Integrating Skills
Grammar
- Types of Pronouns

Preparing to Read
___ Comparing Literature
___ Build Background
___ Focus Your Reading
    Literary Analysis: Imagery   ❑ Unit Seven Resource Book: Literary Analysis SkillBuilder, p. 72
    Active Reading: Analyzing Descriptive Details   ❑ Unit Seven Resource Book: Active Reading SkillBuilder, p. 71

Teaching the Literature
___ Reading the Selection   ❑ PE pp. 1223–1226

Thinking Through the Literature
___ Connect to the Literature
___ Think Critically   ❑ Reading and Critical Thinking Transparencies, T48, T46, T51
___ Extend Interpretations
___ Literary Analysis: Imagery

Choices and Challenges
Writing Options
___ Description of a Place
___ Grocery List
___ Points of Comparison

Activities and Explorations
___ Dramatic Skit
___ Advertising Flyer

Inquiry and Research
___ Latin American Cookbook

Author Activity
___ Poetry Slam

Copyright © McDougal Littell Inc.

Teaching Options (from Teacher's Edition)

Mini Lesson

Grammar

____ Types of Pronouns ❑ Grammar Transparencies and Copymasters, T39, T40, C65

Assessment

____ Selection Test ❑ Formal Assessment: Selection Test, pp. 231–232

____ Test Generator

Homework Assignments
_____
_____
_____
_____
_____

Other Teaching Materials
_____
_____
_____
_____

Copyright © McDougal Littell Inc.

Straw into Gold: The Metamorphosis of the Everyday

Pages 1227–1233

Core Objectives
- Understand and appreciate a personal essay by a Latina writer
- Understand and appreciate voice
- Analyze structure

Integrating Skills

Grammar
- Noun Phrases
- Style: Deliberate Fragments

Vocabulary
- Using Context Clues

Preparing to Read
____ Comparing Literature
____ Build Background
____ Vocabulary Preview: Using Context Clues   ❏ Unit Seven Resource Book: Words to Know SkillBuilder, p. 76
____ Focus Your Reading
      Literary Analysis: Voice   ❏ Unit Seven Resource Book: Literary Analysis SkillBuilder, p. 75
      Active Reading: Analyzing Structure   ❏ Unit Seven Resource Book: Active Reading SkillBuilder, p. 74

Teaching the Literature
                                                                 ❏ PE pp. 1227–1233
____ Reading the Selection   ❏ Unit Seven Resource Book: Summary, p. 73

Thinking Through the Literature
____ Connect to the Literature
____ Think Critically   ❏ Reading and Critical Thinking Transparencies, T15
____ Extend Interpretations
____ Literary Analysis: Voice   ❏ Literary Analysis Transparencies, T23

Choices and Challenges

Writing Options
____ Letter of Advice
____ Points of Comparison

Art Connection
____ *Olga* by Rufino Tomayo

Vocabulary in Action
____ Meaning Clues

Copyright © McDougal Littell Inc.

Straw into Gold: The Metamorphosis of the Everyday

Teaching Options (from Teacher's Edition)

Mini Lessons

Preteaching Vocabulary
____ Using Context Clues

Grammar
____ Noun Phrases   ❏ Grammar Transparencies and Copymasters, C179
____ Style: Deliberate Fragments   ❏ Grammar Transparencies and Copymasters, C180

Viewing and Representing
Art Appreciation
____ *Olga* by Rufino Tamayo

Assessment

____ Selection Quiz   ❏ Formal Assessment: Selection Quiz, p. 77
____ Selection Test   ❏ Formal Assessment: Selection Test, pp 233–234
____ Part Test   ❏ Formal Assessment: Unit Seven, Part 2 Test, pp. 235–236
____ Test Generator

Homework Assignments	Other Teaching Materials

Copyright © McDougal Littell Inc.

Core Objectives

Integrating Skills
Grammar   Vocabulary

Preparing to Read
____ Connect to Your Life
____ Build Background
____ Preteaching Vocabulary
____ Focus Your Reading
Literary Analysis:
Active Reading:

Teaching the Literature
____ Reading the Selection

Thinking Through the Literature
____ Connect to the Literature
____ Think Critically
____ Extend Interpretations
____ Literary Analysis:

Choices and Challenges
____ Writing Options

____ Activities and Explorations

____ Inquiry and Research

____ Vocabulary in Action

____ Grammar in Context

____ Author Activity

____ Art Connection

Copyright © McDougal Littell Inc.

Teaching Options (from Teacher's Edition)

Mini Lessons

Vocabulary Strategy

Speaking and Listening

Viewing and Representing: Art Appreciation

Grammar

Cross Curricular Links

Informal Assessment

Assessment

____ Selection Quiz
____ Selection Test
____ Part Test
____ Test Generator

Homework Assignments	Other Teaching Materials

Copyright © McDougal Littell Inc.

Writing Prompt

Preparing
___ Introduction
___ Basics in a Box
___ Using the Graphic
___ Presenting the Rubric

___ Analyzing a Student Model

Writing
___ Prewriting

___ Drafting

___ Peer Review

___ Revising

___ Editing and Proofreading

___ Reflecting

Homework Assignments	**Other Teaching Materials**
_____	_____
_____	_____
_____	_____
_____	_____

Copyright © McDougal Littell Inc.

CURRICULUM

CURRICULUM

Weeks-Townsend Memorial Library
Union College
Barbourville, KY 40906